POWERPOINT 2003

STEPHEN COPESTAKE

In easy steps is an imprint of Computer Step
Southfield Road . Southam
Warwickshire CV47 0FB . United Kingdom
www.ineasysteps.com

Notice of Liability

Every effort has been made to ensure that this book contains accurate and current information. However, Computer Step and the author shall not be liable for any loss or damage suffered by readers as a result of any information contained herein.

Trademarks

Microsoft® and Windows® are registered trademarks of Microsoft Corporation. All other trademarks are acknowledged as belonging to their respective companies.

Printed and bound in the United Kingdom

ISBN 1-84078-270-6

Contents

Getting acquainted with PowerPoint 2003

Hey, PowerPoint 2003 is really great for creating and presenting slide shows but let's be honest: it's so feature-rich it can be overpowering at first. As a result, this chapter concentrates on giving you an overall flavor of some of the features you'll use frequently. You'll examine the basic screen layout then zero in on key areas like the Task Pane, Smart Tags, slide views, undo/redo, zoom and presentation security. You'll also use Office Online to hook in to Microsoft's online PowerPoint community. Office Online gives you lots of cool stuff like free clip art and training.

Covers

Chapter One

The PowerPoint 2003 screen

When you've told PowerPoint 2003 to create a new presentation based on a template or with the help of the AutoContent Wizard (see Chapter 2), or if you've chosen to open an existing presentation, the final result will look something like this:

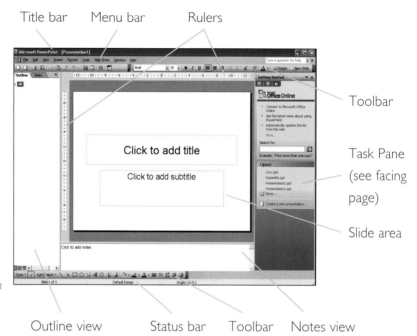

Title bar   Menu bar   Rulers

Toolbar

Task Pane (see facing page)

Slide area

Where Outline view is currently displayed you can also display Thumbnail view.

Outline view   Status bar   Toolbar   Notes view

This, however, is simply one "view": Normal view. PowerPoint 2003 lets you interact with presentations in various ways. It does this by providing the following additional major views:

- Outline
- Slide Sorter
- Notes Page

See pages 10 thru 12 later for more information.

An additional view (Slide Show) displays your presentation the way its eventual audience will watch it. See Chapter 9 for more information on Slide Show view.

The PowerPoint Task Pane

PowerPoint 2003 provides a special pane on the right of the screen which you can use to launch various tasks. Some of the main incarnations of the Task Pane are:

The use of the Task Pane is also covered at appropriate locations throughout this book.

- New Presentation

- Clipboard

- Search Results

- Research

- Clip Art

To display or hide the Task Pane, pull down the View menu and click Task Pane.

You also use Task Panes to apply designs, layouts and animations.

Using the Task Pane

If no Task Pane is visible, hit Ctrl+F1

If you're new to PowerPoint, get familiar with the Task Pane as quickly as you can: you'll be using it a lot.

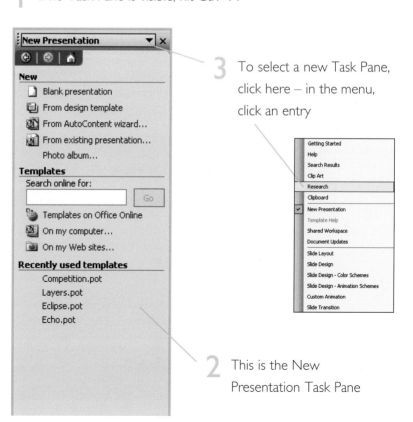

3 To select a new Task Pane, click here – in the menu, click an entry

2 This is the New Presentation Task Pane

The slide views – an overview

Views described

PowerPoint has several views which you should use for differing purposes:

Normal (or Tri-Pane) view

Each slide displays individually, with the maximum detail.

Normal view includes the following additional features:

There are also various Master views – see Chapter 3 for how to use these.

- Outline pane – shows the textual structure underlying slides

- Slides pane – shows each slide as a thumbnail (as in Slide Sorter view)

- Notes view – shows the speaker notes associated with the active slide

Slide Sorter view

All the slides display as icons so you can use them more easily.

Notes Page view

Each slide displays, together with any speaker notes.

Certain view-related changes (such as amendments to the Outline pane) are saved with the host presentation. However, if you want to specify the view that PowerPoint launches by default, hit Tools, Options. Select the View tab then, under Default view, select the view you need.

These are different ways of looking at your slide show. Normal view provides a very useful overview, while Slide Sorter view lets you modify more than one slide at a time.

These views are also discussed in later chapters.

Switching to a view

1. Pull down the View menu and select a view

2. In Normal view, to move between the Outline and Slides panes, hit Ctrl+Shift+Tab

3. To select Normal or Slide Sorter view, hit either of these icons on the bottom left of the PowerPoint screen:

Normal

Slide

Sorter

Using the slide views

Here are some additional tips on how best to use views.

Normal view

Normal view displays the current slide in its own window. Use Normal view when you want a detailed picture of a slide (for instance, when you amend any of the slide contents, or when you change the overall formatting). Normal view is your main way to create and design slides.

1 Select a tab here to view slides in the Outline pane (you can amend this and watch your changes take effect in the Slide area on the right) or in the Slides pane

To enlarge or shrink the Outline/Slides view, drag its splitter bar.

To jump to the next or earlier slide, press Page Down or Page Up respectively.

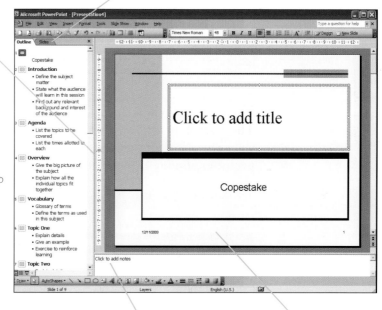

2 Enter speaker notes   Slide area

Slide Sorter view

If you need to rearrange the order of slides, use Slide Sorter view. You can simply click on a slide and drag it to a new location (to move more than one slide, hold down one Ctrl key as you click them, then release the key and drag). You can also copy a slide by holding down Ctrl as you drag.

You can also use Slide Sorter view to apply a new slide layout to more than one slide at a time – see page 39.

 Slide Sorter view gives you a useful overview – use it near the end of the slide show creation process to verify everything is as you want it.

 In Normal and Notes Page views, you can also use the vertical scroll bar to move to specific slides. As you drag the bar, PowerPoint shows a message telling you the number and title of the slide you're at.

To perform additional operations, right-click any slide and select an entry in the shortcut menu

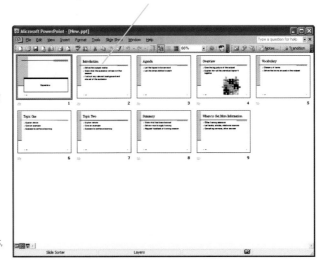

Slide Sorter view

Notes Page view

This view is an aid to the presenter rather than the viewer of the slide show. If you want to enter speaker notes on a slide (for later printing), use Notes Page view.

The slide is displayed at a reduced size

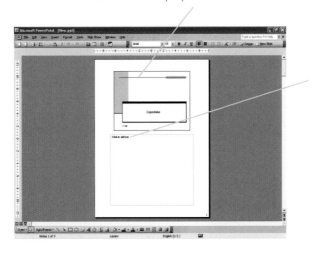

Enter notes – see Chapter 7. (You can also do this in Normal view)

Working with toolbars

Toolbars are important components in PowerPoint 2003. A toolbar is an onscreen bar which contains shortcut buttons. These symbolize and allow easy access to often-used commands which would normally have to be invoked via one or more menus.

For example, PowerPoint 2003's Standard toolbar lets you:

- create, open, save and print presentations

- perform copy & paste and cut & paste operations

- undo editing actions

- launch the Research Task Pane

You can create your own toolbar. Right-click any toolbar and hit Customize. In the Customize dialog, select the Toolbars tab and hit New. Name the toolbar and allocate a template.

by simply clicking on the relevant button.

We'll be looking at toolbars in more detail as we encounter them. For the moment, some general advice:

Specifying which toolbars are displayed

Choose View, Toolbars

You can't rename any of the toolbars that come with PowerPoint.

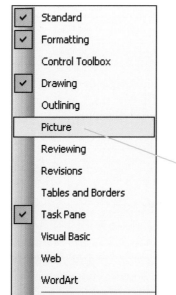

The Task Pane is a toolbar. To hide or show it, uncheck or check the Task Pane entry on the right.

2 Check the toolbar you want to be visible – repeat as necessary

3 You can also right-click any existing toolbar and check or uncheck any entry in the shortcut menu

Automatic customization

Menus and toolbars are personalized in PowerPoint 2003.

Submenus aren't customized.

Personalized menus

When you first use PowerPoint 2003, its menus display the features which Microsoft believes are used 95% of the time and features which are infrequently used are not immediately visible. This makes for less cluttered screens.

Personalizing menus is made clear in the illustrations below:

PowerPoint menus expand automatically, after a slight delay. However, to expand them manually, click the chevrons at the bottom of the menu.

PowerPoint 2003's Tools menu, as it first appears...

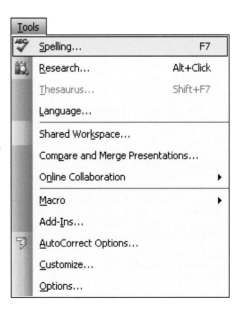

Automatic customization also applies to toolbars. Note the following:

- *if possible, they display on a single row*
- *they overlap when there isn't enough room onscreen*
- *icons are "promoted" and "demoted" like menu entries*
- *demoted icons are shown in a separate fly-out, reached by clicking:*

...the expanded menu. (As you use PowerPoint, individual features are dynamically promoted or demoted. This means menus are continually evolving)

Undo and Redo

PowerPoint lets you reverse – "undo" – just about any editing operation. If, subsequently, you decide that you do want to proceed with an operation that you've reversed, you can "redo" it. You can also undo or redo a series of operations in one go.

You can undo and redo actions in the following ways:

Using the keyboard

You can undo most changes to images by clicking the Reset Picture button in the Picture toolbar.

1 Press Ctrl+Z to undo an action

2 Press Ctrl+Y to reinstate it

Using the Edit menu

The AutoCorrect button also lets you undo certain actions like automated capitalizations. See page 19.

1 Choose Edit, Undo...

2 Or choose Edit, Redo...

The dots denote the action being reversed or undone.

Using the Standard toolbar

1 Click here to undo the last action

2 Or click here to redo the last action

3 To undo or redo multiple actions, click the arrow to the right of the Undo or Redo buttons

4 In the list, select 1 or more operations. If you select an early operation in the list (i.e. one near the bottom), all later operations are included

Using Zoom

It's often useful to be able to zoom in or out on your slides. You can zoom in and out in any PowerPoint 2003 view (although the available options vary).

Setting the Zoom level

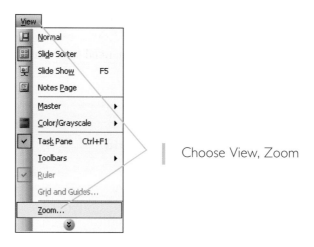

Choose View, Zoom

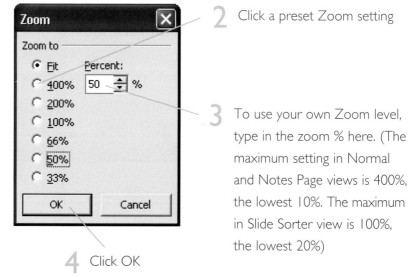

If Fit is available, click it to redisplay the entire slide.

2 Click a preset Zoom setting

3 To use your own Zoom level, type in the zoom % here. (The maximum setting in Normal and Notes Page views is 400%, the lowest 10%. The maximum in Slide Sorter view is 100%, the lowest 20%)

4 Click OK

5 You can also use another technique to set Zoom levels. Just click the Zoom button 100% in the Standard toolbar and select a level in the drop-down list

Using Smart Tags

PowerPoint 2003 recognizes certain types of data and flags them with a purple underline. When you move the mouse pointer over the line, an "action button" appears that provides access to commands that would otherwise have to be accessed from menus, toolbars or other programs. Smart Tags are data-specific labels.

There are several types of Smart Tag in PowerPoint 2003. These include Person Names from Outlook Contact lists or from recent email recipients and financial symbols.

Using Smart Tags

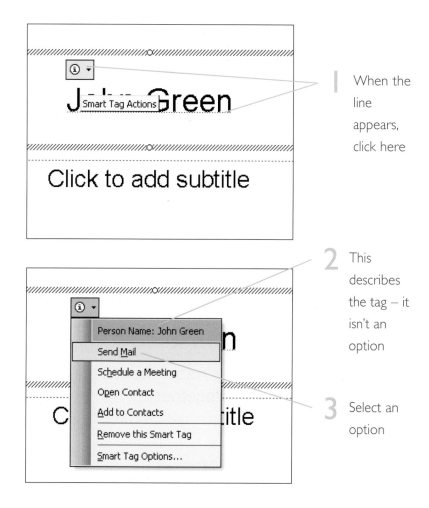

1 When the line appears, click here

2 This describes the tag – it isn't an option

3 Select an option

PowerPoint also uses additional action buttons that resemble Smart Tags in the way they work.

The Paste Options button

In Slide Sorter view, a slide has been pasted after a slide that has a different design template

The Paste Options button also appears when you paste in text and tables.

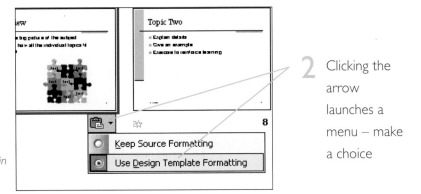

2 Clicking the arrow launches a menu – make a choice

The AutoFit Options button

If the text you insert in a text placeholder is too big, PowerPoint automatically resizes it

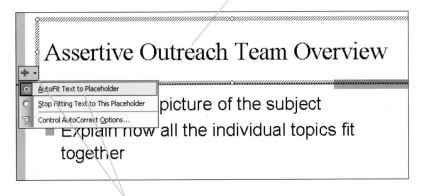

2 Clicking the arrow launches a menu – make a choice

The AutoCorrect button

PowerPoint's AutoCorrect feature (see Chapter 2) uses a special button to give you the option of canceling the change.

1 Whenever an automatic correction occurs (for example, the capitalization of initial letters or the conversion of Web addresses to hyperlinks), move the mouse pointer over it until a small blue box appears

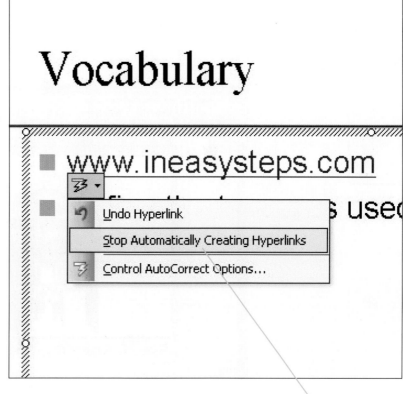

One further button – the Automatic Layout Options button – appears when you insert an item such as a picture, diagram or chart and this changes the slide layout. (To disable this feature, hit Tools, AutoCorrect Options then uncheck "Automatic layout for inserted objects" under the "AutoFormat as you type" tab.)

2 Clicking the box launches a menu – make a choice

Collect and Paste

You can copy multiple items to the Office Clipboard from within any Windows program which supports copy-and-paste but you can only paste in the last one.

If you want to copy-and-paste multiple items of text and/or pictures into a presentation, you can copy as many as 24 items. These are stored in a special version of the Windows Clipboard called the Office Clipboard that in turn is located in the Task Pane. The Office Clipboard displays a visual representation of the data, so it's easy to use.

Using the Office Clipboard
Use standard procedures to copy multiple examples of data and/or pictures – after the first copy, the Clipboard should appear in the Task Pane. Then:

To call up the Office Clipboard at any time, pull down the Edit menu and click Office Clipboard.

Click the data you want to insert
– it appears at the insertion point

If the Clipboard Task Pane persistently refuses to appear after pasting, call it up manually and hit the Options button. Check Show Office Clipboard Automatically.

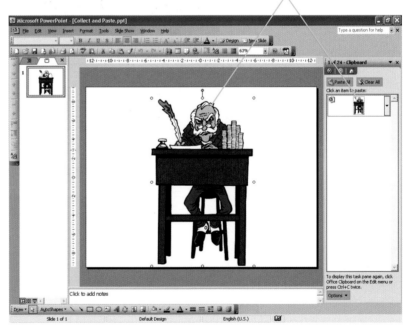

You must use the technique shown here to paste from the Office Clipboard: the normal paste commands like Ctrl+V only paste from the standard Windows Clipboard.

2 If you're inserting text, a Smart Tag appears

3 To clear the contents of the Office Clipboard, click the Clear All button (or close PowerPoint and any other Office modules you may be running at the time)

Quick File Switching

In the past, only programs (not individual windows within programs) displayed on the Windows Taskbar. With PowerPoint 2003, however, all open windows display as separate buttons.

In the following example, four new presentations have been created in PowerPoint 2003. All four display as separate windows, although only one copy of PowerPoint 2003 is running:

Four PowerPoint 2003 windows

This is clarified by a glance at PowerPoint 2003's Window menu which (as before) shows all open PowerPoint windows:

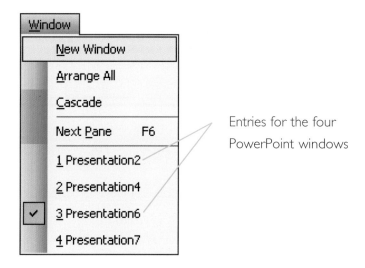

Entries for the four PowerPoint windows

1   To go to a presentation window, simply click its Taskbar button

2   Find Quick File Switching annoying? No problem. To disable it, choose Tools, Options. Select the View tab and uncheck Windows in Taskbar

Repairing errors

PowerPoint 2003 provides a special feature you can use to repair its installation.

Detect and Repair fixes Registry errors and missing files; it will not repair damaged presentations. If the process doesn't work, reinstall PowerPoint 2003.

Detect and Repair

Do the following to correct program errors (but note selecting "Discard my customized settings and restore default settings" in step 2 will ensure that all default PowerPoint settings are restored, so any you've customized – including menu/toolbar positions and view settings – will be lost):

1 Choose Help, Detect and Repair

2 Select one or both options

3 Click here

4 Follow the onscreen instructions – Detect and Repair can be a lengthy process

5 You may have to re-enter your user name and initials when you restart your Office applications

You can also use a further procedure for instances when PowerPoint "hangs" (ceases to respond).

Application Recovery

When errors occur, PowerPoint should give you the option of saving open files before it closes.

1 Click Start, All Programs, Microsoft Office, Microsoft Office Tools, Microsoft Office Application Recovery

2 Select Microsoft Office PowerPoint

You should make sure AutoRecover is turned on to make it easier to recover presentations. Choose Tools, Options. Select the Save tab and check "Save AutoRecover info every...". Set an AutoRecover interval.

3 Click Recover Application to have PowerPoint try to recover the presentation(s) you were working on

4 Decide whether to email error details to Microsoft

5 PowerPoint opens with the Getting Started Task Pane. Click the file you want to reopen

Using Office Online

Imagine a scenario. You're sitting at your desk, working on a killer PowerPoint spreadsheet, when you hit a problem. Let's say there's a key program area you need help with, like using slide masters to insert content on multiple slides or finding a specific piece of information that would go really well in a slide. Or maybe something just isn't working the way it should. Apart from saying "Oh heck" (or words to that effect), what do you do?

There are two things you do. First, you don't panic. Second, you use Office Online to find the answer you need.

Office Online is a special website which provides dedicated resources that are updated regularly in line with user feedback. There are links to Office Online in various of the Task Panes and menus you'll meet as you work thru this book. Office Online gives you helpful articles, templates, clips and training links, organized into several key areas.

A lot of the help that Microsoft provides is only available on the Web, so it pays to use Office Online.

Key areas

Office Online has several key areas. Use the following as guides (but bear in mind of course that aspects of Office Online may have changed by the time you read this):

- Assistance – hints and tips. Also provides PowerPoint-specific help

- Training – links to tutorials

- Templates – lots of templates and some downloads

- Clip Art and Media – clips organized under headings

- Downloads – access to popular downloads and a link to Windows Update

- Office Marketplace – showcases related non-Microsoft products and services

- Product Information – additional services

Connecting to Office Online

1 The Getting Started Task Pane launches when you start PowerPoint 2003. If it isn't visible, hit Ctrl+F1 then select it in the drop-down list

2 With your Internet connection live, click here then follow steps 4 thru 6 overleaf

3 Alternatively, click here to jump straight to the PowerPoint section of Office Online's Assistance key area (lots of useful links here)

4 Select an area then any link

You can also use the Research Task Pane to carry out research – see page 64.

5 Or search for what you want

6 If you carried out a search, click a link

Getting help from within PowerPoint

Type in your question in the Ask a Question box and press Enter

If you'd rather use Office Online directly to get help, you can hide the Ask a Question box to make more room onscreen. Choose Tools, Customize. Right-click the box and uncheck "Show Ask a Question box". Hit Close.

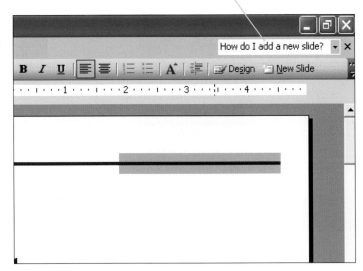

3 Or power up your Web connection and click here to launch Office Online

2 The Search Results Task Pane launches. Click any relevant entry (especially, click Knowledge Base Search to hunt thru the Microsoft Knowledge Base, a vast repository of problem-solving solutions)

Alternatively, press F1

If your Internet connection is live, step 2 searches Office Online.

2 Type in search text (optimally, 2–7 words) then hit the arrow

3 Instead, fire up Office Online directly or select a specific link (Assistance, Training and Downloads are Office Online areas. Hit Communities for access to Office-specific forums)

4 After step 2, select a link in the Search Results pane

The Knowledge Base is a vast store of informational material and articles that Microsoft maintains for the benefit of users. You're almost certain to find what you need there.

5 Or (with your Internet connection live) hit a suggestion. Try Knowledge Base Search if you need detailed help – Research refers to the Research Task Pane

Making presentations secure

You can password-protect your presentations in two ways:

Make a written note of your password and keep it safe. If you lose it, you won't be able to access your presentation.

- on an open basis, where users need a password to open a presentation

- on a use basis, where users need a password to amend a presentation (without the password, they can still view it and/or save it to another name)

Setting a password

If you need really long passwords (up to 255 characters), hit the Advanced button. Select an encryption type then choose the number of characters you need in the "Choose a key length" box.

1 Pull down the Tools menu and select Options

2 Ensure the Security tab is active

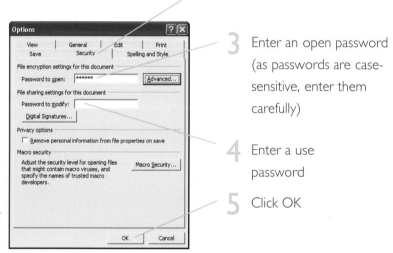

3 Enter an open password (as passwords are case-sensitive, enter them carefully)

4 Enter a use password

5 Click OK

You should give serious thought to the password you choose. For example, all passwords should consist of an easily memorable combination of upper- and lower-case letters, symbols, spaces and numerals. P89aL $43X would be an effective password (if you could recall it) while Opensesame8 definitely wouldn't.

6 Reiterate your password(s) then click OK

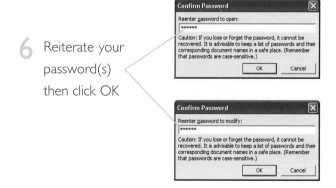

Opening password-protected presentations

1 Follow the relevant procedures to open a presentation

2 PowerPoint 2003 launches a special dialog. Do the following:

As a way of controlling sensitive information, you can use a new feature called Information Rights Management to restrict access to sensitive presentations (but only if you're using Microsoft Office Professional Edition 2003 or the standalone version of PowerPoint 2003). You do this via the Permission dialog box – File, Permission, Do Not Distribute.

You may have to download and install the Windows Rights Management client before you can proceed.

3 Type in the password you set in step 3 on page 29

4 Click OK

Amending password-protected presentations

1 If you also set an open password, follow steps 1–4 above. If not, merely follow step 1

*Want to know more about Information Rights Management? Open Office Online's Assistance pane and look for **Introducing Information Rights Management**.*

*There is also a free trial IRM service. Open the same pane and search for **Free Trial Service for Information Rights Management**.*

2 Type in the password you set in step 4 on page 29

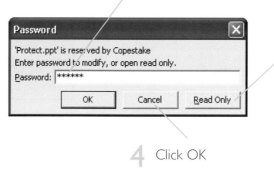

3 Or hit Read Only if you don't want to amend the presentation

4 Click OK

Creating and developing slide shows

There are lots of ways to create slide shows and this chapter explores them all. Once you've gotten your own, enhance it with layouts and text and add bullets and formatting for more impact. Text errors are corrected automatically but any that slip thru can be remedied via a quick spell-check. The Outline tab provides a text overview and you can use the Research Task Pane to find synonyms, translate text and do in-slide research.

Once you've gotten your presentation just the way you want it, why not publish it to the Web?

Covers

Chapter Two

Creating slide shows – an overview

PowerPoint 2003 lets you create a new presentation in the following ways (in descending order of ease of use):

- the "suggested content" route (with the help of the AutoContent Wizard)

You can also create new slide shows directly from existing ones. Launch the New Presentation Task Pane. Select "From existing presentation" then double-click a presentation. Make the relevant changes then save the presentation to a new name.

- by basing it on a template, and creating each slide and its contents (apart from the background) manually

- by creating a blank presentation, and creating each slide and its contents (including the background) manually

The AutoContent Wizard

The AutoContent Wizard is a high-powered yet easy-to-use shortcut to creating a slide show. It incorporates a question-and-answer system. You work through a series of dialogs, answering the appropriate questions and making the relevant choices. This is the easiest way to produce a slide show, but the results are nonetheless highly professional. You get presentations with lots of content – it's usually easier to change this than insert your own.

Templates

Templates – also known as boilerplates – are sample presentations, complete with the relevant formatting and/or text. By basing a new slide show on a template, you automatically have access to these. Templates don't offer as many formatting choices as the AutoContent Wizard, but the results are just as professional. Again, you can customize them as much as you want.

Obviously, you can use any templates that are on your hard disk and/or network but you're not limited to these: Office Online provides lots of additional ones that are easy to access and use.

Blank presentations

Creating blank presentations is the simplest route; use this if you want to define the slide show components yourself from scratch. This is often not the most efficient or effective way to create new presentations. However, it isn't as difficult as you might imagine because PowerPoint 2003 lets you apply predefined slide layouts (to individual slides) and slide designs based on templates (see Chapter 3).

Using the AutoContent Wizard

PowerPoint 2003 has a unique and particularly detailed Wizard which handles the basics of creating a presentation.

Creating a slide show via the AutoContent Wizard

This is probably the best way to produce a new presentation. The Wizard produces a "standard" slide show which you can amend later, largely by applying a new design or layout.

1 If the Task Pane isn't already onscreen, hit Ctrl+F1

PowerPoint presentations don't just run onscreen: you can also opt to create Web and various kinds of overhead presentations.

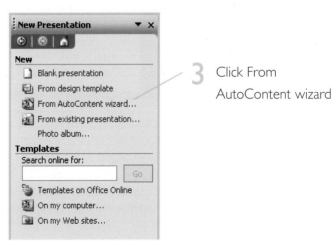

2 In the Getting Started Task Pane, click Create a new presentation

3 Click From AutoContent wizard

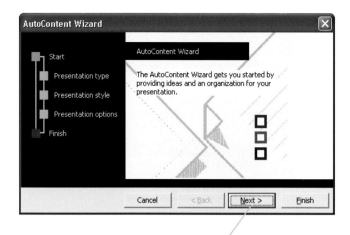

4 Click here to begin working with the Wizard

5 Select a presentation type or hit All to view every type

6 Select a presentation

The AutoContent Wizard uses content templates. These are design templates with the addition of a suggested outline.

To add your own template to the wizard, click Add. Use the Select Presentation Template dialog to locate and double-click the relevant template. (Or get rid of a template by selecting it in the dialog and hitting Remove.)

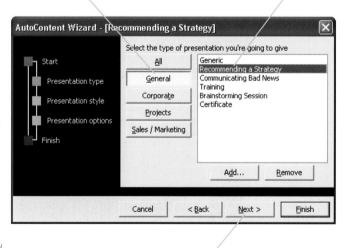

7 Click Next to move on

8 Select an output type

There are several types of presentation – select the one you need. "On-screen presentation" is the option you'll likely use the most. The "Web presentation" option applies a color scheme that is suitable for use on the Internet or intranets.

9 Click here

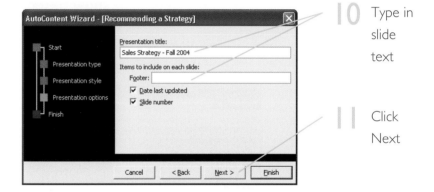

10 Type in slide text

11 Click Next

12 Hit Finish in the next screen to generate the presentation:

Replacing the template text with your own is absolutely all you need to do to achieve a professional presentation – it's that easy. Of course, you can make it even better with some judicious customization . . .

Using templates

When you create a slide show with the help of a template, you:

1. select a template

2. apply a pre-defined layout

3. type in your text (and/or add pictures, org charts and graphs)

PowerPoint calls these templates "design templates". These are the same as the content templates used by the AutoContent Wizard with one exception: content templates also have a suggested text outline.

Step 1 applies to the overall presentation, while steps 2 and 3 have to be applied to selected slides. This makes creating new presentations based on templates a rather longer process than using the AutoContent Wizard. However, the end result is likely to be more personalized and it is easier to have variations in individual style layout, if you need this.

For more on using design templates, see pages 77 and 86 in Chapter 3.

Creating a new slide show based on a template

Pull down the File menu and click New

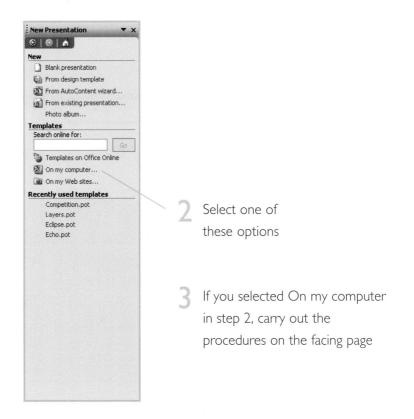

2 Select one of these options

3 If you selected On my computer in step 2, carry out the procedures on the facing page

4 Click this tab   **6** Preview templates

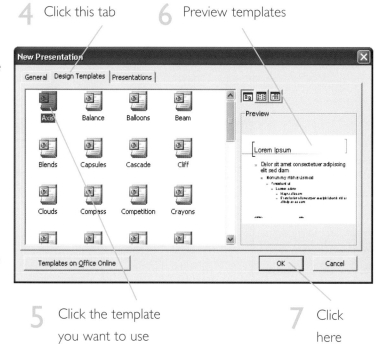

5 Click the template you want to use   **7** Click here

8 Follow the on-screen instructions:

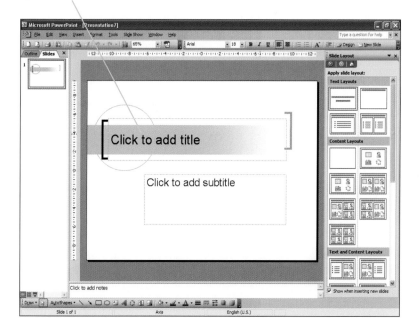

9 If you selected Templates on Office Online in step 2 on page 36 (for more on Office Online, see also pages 24 thru 26), click Presentations then download and use any of the supplied templates

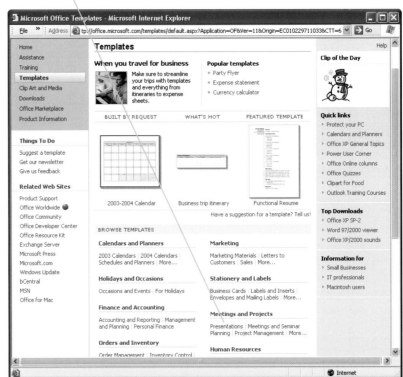

You can create your own templates for future use. When saved, they appear in the Slide Design Task Pane (Format, Slide Design) after you've restarted PowerPoint.

Open the slide show you want to preserve. Choose File, Save As. In the Save as type: field, select Design Template (*.pot). Select a drive/folder then name the template. Click Save.

10 If you selected On my Web sites in step 2, use the dialog that launches to search for templates on your networked websites

Applying a layout to the new slide show

The standard layout which PowerPoint automatically applies to your new presentation may not be suitable – for example, it may not have a picture placeholder. You can easily apply a different one.

Layouts are less complex than templates. Basically, they just relate to the way items on your slides are organized. If a slide has a suitable layout, it's much easier to fine-tune it so it does what you want.

It's sometimes useful to apply a blank layout to a slide – that way, you can easily add as many or as few items as you need and customize them.

Don't feel a slide's placeholders restrict the way you develop the slide: you can add as many extra items as you like. When you do this, PowerPoint inserts new placeholders and automatically adjust the slide layout.

Don't like the new look? No problem: just use the Automatic Layout Options button (on the bottom right of the slide) to undo it. Or turn off this feature – hit Tools, AutoCorrect Options, select the AutoFormat As You Type tab and uncheck "Automatic layout for inserted objects".

1 If you selected On my computer in step 2 on page 36, the Slide Layout Task Pane will automatically be onscreen. If not, launch it

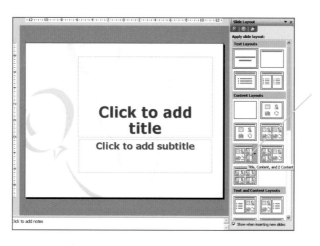

2 To apply a different slide layout, click it

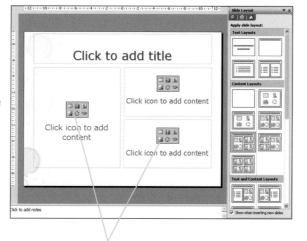

You use placeholders to add charts, clip art, pictures and other media clips

3 This new layout has lots of extra placeholders

4 Rearrange, resize or format the placeholders as appropriate

Creating blank slide shows

1   Hit File, New

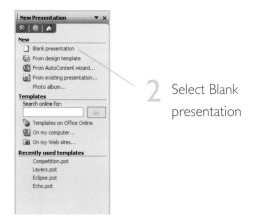

2   Select Blank presentation

3   Select a layout for the single slide the new presentation contains

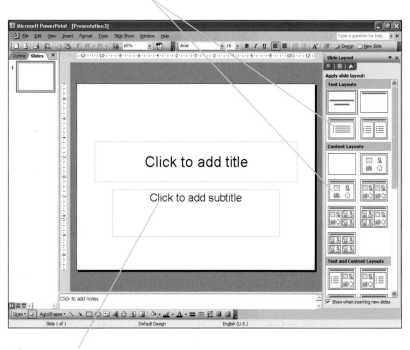

After step 5, add layouts if required.

4   Using any text placeholders, type in the necessary text

5   Create any new slides required (see the facing page)

Creating additional slides

Obviously, you'll want to add (then customize) your own new slides, irrespective of how you created your presentation. Hey, nothing could be easier.

1 To create a new slide based on the template you selected in step 5 on page 37, pull down the Insert menu and hit New Slide

2 Alternatively, just press Ctrl+M (but don't confuse this with the Ctrl+N command that launches a whole new blank presentation)

3 You can use another route. In the Formatting toolbar, hit this button: New Slide

4 If you carried out step 1, 2 or 3, follow the procedures on page 39 to assign a slide layout

5 You can insert slides from an external slide show into the active presentation. Select the slide you want to precede the new one and hit Insert, Slides from Files. Use the Slide Finder to locate the presentation you want to copy from then specify the relevant slides. Click Insert (or Insert All to insert all slides)

Saving even more time

6 You can create a slide and apply a layout in one go. In the Slide Layout Task Pane (Format, Slide Layout), click the arrow of the layout you want the slide to have then select Insert New Slide

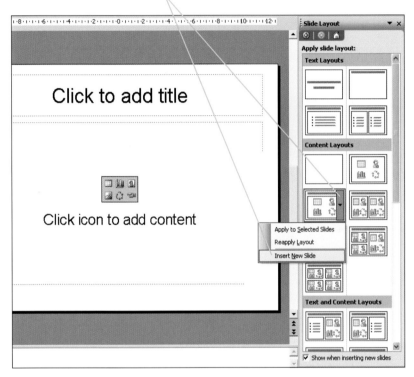

7 You can also use another method if you're working with a presentation's outline: with the cursor in the slide's first entry, just press Enter to create a new slide

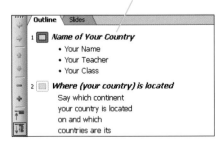

Adding text to slides

When you create a new slide show, PowerPoint 2003 fills each slide with placeholders containing sample text. The idea is that you should replace this with your own text.

Don't forget you can enter text directly into the Outline tab in Normal view – see pages 54 thru 57.

You can also add text to AutoShapes (see page 100).

Inserting text into a text placeholder is a shortcut to the creation of a text box.

When you enter text into a placeholder, PowerPoint 2003 resizes it to fit by altering the line spacing, the type size or both. Click the AutoFit Options button to undo the resizing.

Text in text boxes does not appear in the Outline tab.

1 Click in a placeholder

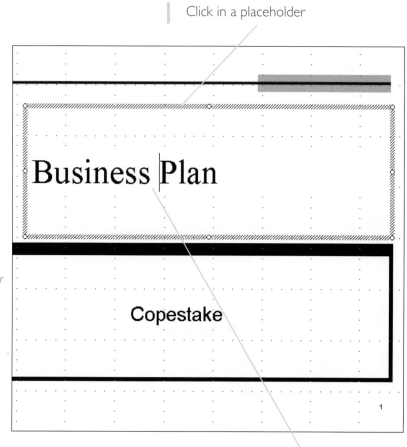

2 PowerPoint displays a text entry box – type in your own text

3 Click anywhere outside the placeholder to confirm the addition of the new text

4 Alternatively, click this button in the Drawing toolbar: then drag out a text box anywhere on a slide and insert the necessary text (see also page 48)

Using grids

You can add a grid to slides within Normal or Notes Page views. This is a useful feature because you can align objects such as pictures to it.

Enabling the grid

1 In Normal or Notes Page view, pull down the View menu and select Grid and Guides

Ensure Snap objects to grid is checked to have objects "attracted" to the grid.

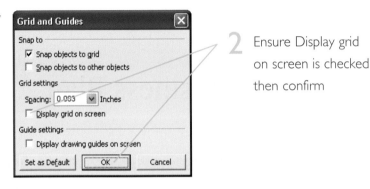

2 Ensure Display grid on screen is checked then confirm

You can also apply manual ("drawing") guides. Ensure "Display drawing guides on screen" is checked. When you close the dialog, 1 horizontal and 1 vertical line appear on-screen; drag these to a new location and align objects with them.

The grid structure

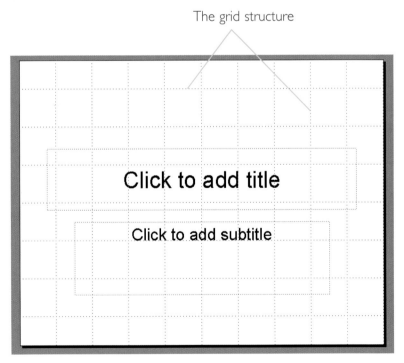

Click to add title

Click to add subtitle

AutoCorrect – an overview

If you're not too hot at typing or spelling, PowerPoint's AutoCorrect feature is a real boon. Its principal purpose is to correct typing errors automatically. It does this by maintaining a list of inaccurate spellings and word forms and their corrected versions. When you press the Spacebar or Enter/Return keys immediately after making a mistake, it's corrected automatically. Neat, huh?

AutoCorrect is supplied with a long list of preset corrections. Some common examples are:

In operation, AutoCorrect uses the Smart Tag-like AutoCorrect button – see page 19 for how to use this.

- *allwasy* and *allwyas* become *always*

- *acomodate* and *acommodate* become *accommodate*

- *alot* becomes *a lot*

- *dont* becomes *don't*

- *garantee* becomes *guarantee*

- *oppertunity* becomes *opportunity*

- *wierd* becomes *weird*

AutoCorrect also routinely replaces *(c)*, *(r)* and *(tm)* with ©, ® and ™. This is much easier than using the Windows Character Map.

In addition, however, you can easily define your own. If, for instance, you regularly type "lthe" when you mean "the", you can have AutoCorrect make the correction for you.

You can also enter shortened forms of correct words – or entire phrases – and have them expanded automatically. (For instance, you could have AutoCorrect expand "ann" into "Annual Profit Forecast".)

Even better
AutoCorrect has further uses. You can have:

1. the first letters of sentences capitalized

2. words that begin with two capitals corrected (e.g. *HEllo* becomes *Hello*)

3. days capitalized (e.g. *monday* becomes *Monday*)

Customizing AutoCorrect

You can add new corrections, change or delete existing ones and specify which AutoCorrect functions are active.

Adding new corrections

1 Hit Tools, AutoCorrect Options

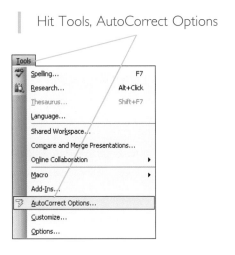

If you don't want errors corrected automatically, uncheck "Replace text as you type".

To redefine an existing entry, select it in the list, overtype new details then hit Replace. Click Yes in the confirmatory box.

To remove an entry, select it here then click the Delete button. PowerPoint 2003 deletes the item immediately.

2 Select the AutoCorrect tab

3 Type in the incorrect word

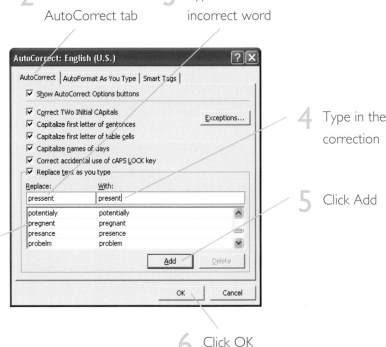

4 Type in the correction

5 Click Add

6 Click OK

Setting other AutoCorrect options

I Launch the AutoCorrect dialog (see the facing page) then select the AutoCorrect tab

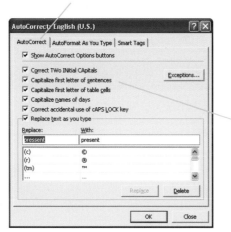

2 Uncheck any of these options then hit OK

You can also specify exceptions to the rule whereby double capitals at the start of words are corrected. For example, the plural of the abbreviation PA (for Personal Assistant) is "PAs". Clearly, for PowerPoint to correct this to "Pas" would be wrong.

Select the INitial CAps tab. Enter the exception in the Don't correct field and click Add. Click OK twice.

Specifying exceptions

There are situations where automatic capitalization is wrong. For instance, if you type in *approx.* followed by another word, the first letter of the second word is incorrectly capitalized due to the preceding period. To prevent this, you can set up an exception.

I In the above dialog, click the Exceptions button

2 Select the First Letter tab

3 Type in an exception

This dialog does not distinguish between lower- and upper-case. For example, entering "quart." has the same effect as entering "Quart." or "QUART.".

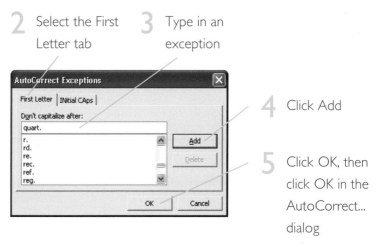

4 Click Add

5 Click OK, then click OK in the AutoCorrect... dialog

Inserting text boxes

If a slide contains no text placeholders (or even if it does), you can still insert text easily and conveniently by creating and inserting a text box.

Text boxes are great for inserting captions or annotating charts.

Creating a text box

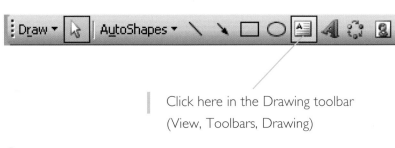

1 Click here in the Drawing toolbar (View, Toolbars, Drawing)

2 Drag to define the text box

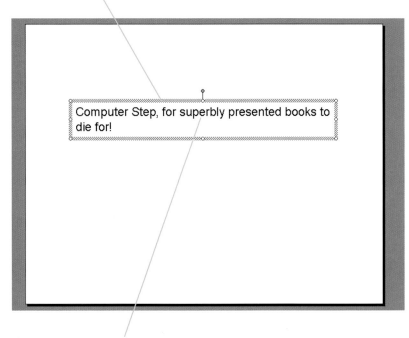

Computer Step, for superbly presented books to die for!

3 Type in the relevant text. Click outside the box when you're thru

Formatting text

Font-based formatting

You need to format text, so it does just what you want with the maximum impact.

1 Click inside the relevant text object and select the text you want to format

2 Hit Ctrl+T then carry out any of steps 3 thru 8 below, as appropriate. Finally, follow step 9

You can replace fonts globally. Choose Format, Replace Fonts. Specify the old and new font and hit Replace.

3 Select a typeface

4 Type in a new point size

9 Click here

7 Click here then follow step 8

5 Select one or more effects

6 Click a font style to apply it

8 Click a color. If none are suitable, click More Colors and select one in the new dialog

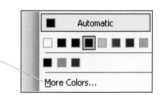

Changing text alignment

It's often more convenient to use keyboard alignment shortcuts:

Ctrl+L   Left-align
Ctrl+E   Center-align
Ctrl+R   Right-align

1 Click inside the relevant text object and select the text whose alignment you want to amend

2 Pull down the Format menu and click Alignment. In the submenu, select an alignment

Changing text spacing

1 Click inside the relevant text object and select the text whose spacing you want to amend

2 Pull down the Format menu and click Line Spacing

3 Type in a line spacing

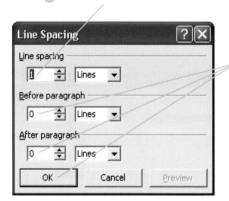

4 Enter a pre- or post-paragraph spacing then click OK

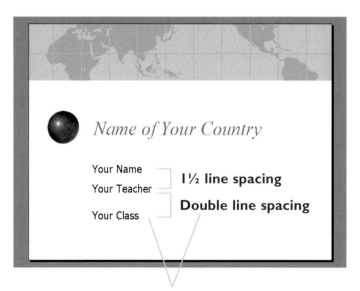

Line spacing in action

Applying tabs

1 Ensure the ruler is visible (View, Ruler) then click inside the relevant text object

2 Click where you want the tab stop to appear

Inserting tabs is a great way to increase text legibility.

To delete a tab stop, simply drag it (the "L" shape) off the ruler.

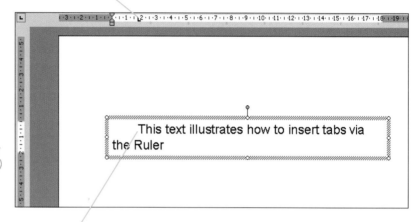

This text illustrates how to insert tabs via the Ruler

3 Back in the text, click where you want the tab to take effect and press the Tab key

Applying indents

1 Ensure the ruler is visible (View, Ruler) then click inside the relevant text object

Never use the Space bar to indent text: spaces give uneven results because they vary in size according to the typeface and type size applying.

2 Drag this to revise the first-line indent

A customized tab stop (to clear it, drag it off the Ruler)

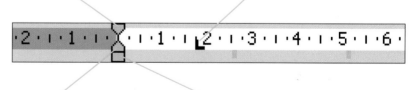

3 Drag this to revise the left indent

4 Drag this to revise the indent for all lines equally

Bulleting text

Text in slides is often bulleted, for increased impact:

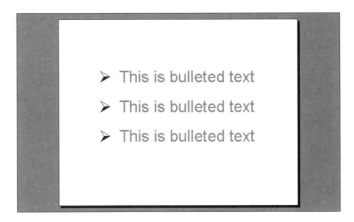

You can adjust bullet/number indents by dragging the appropriate indent marker in the Ruler. For example, to only adjust the bullet or number, drag the first-line market. To adjust the text position relative to the bullet/ number, drag the left indent marker. To adjust the bullet and text together, drag the square marker at the bottom.

Adding bullets to text

1 Click in the relevant text block and select the text you want to reformat

2 Pull down the Format menu and click Bullets and Numbering

3 Activate the Bulleted tab

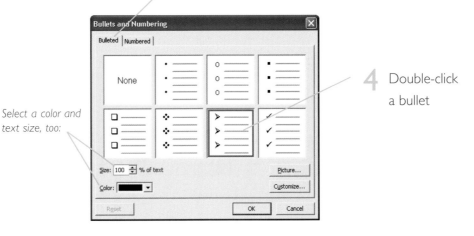

4 Double-click a bullet

Select a color and text size, too:

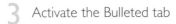

5 To start a new unbulleted/unnumbered line, press Shift+Enter

Customizing bullets

Don't like the standard bullets? No problem – create your own:

1 Launch the Bullets and Numbering dialog (see the facing page) then hit the Customize button

2 Select a font (favorite candidates are **Webdings**, **Wingdings** and ZapfDingbats BT)

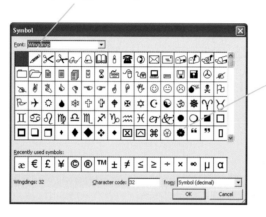

3 Double-click the character you want to bulletize

Numbering text

Numbering lists is good, too:

1 Launch the Bullets and Numbering dialog (see the facing page) then hit the Numbered tab

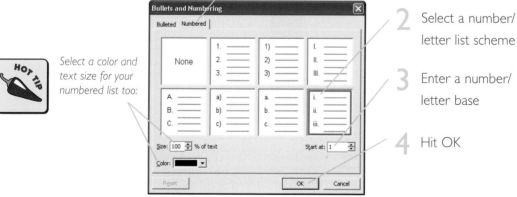

Select a color and text size for your numbered list too:

2 Select a number/ letter list scheme

3 Enter a number/ letter base

4 Hit OK

HOT TIP

Working with slide outlines

You can use the Outline tab in Normal view (Outline view) to organize and develop the content of your presentation.

In Outline view, you can:

- build presentation structures

- move entire slides from one position to another

- edit text entries

- hide or display text levels

When you create a presentation with the AutoContent Wizard, an outline is automatically created for you.

Creating a presentation structure

1   Create a blank presentation or one based on a design template then go to Normal view (View, Normal)

2   Ensure the Outline tab is active then click a slide entry

Want text formatting to display in the Outline pane? Toggle this button in the Standard toolbar:

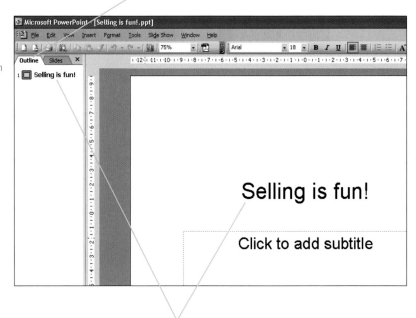

3   Type in title text and press Enter (the change is reflected in the slide itself) to create a new slide – we'll then convert this to a level in the first slide

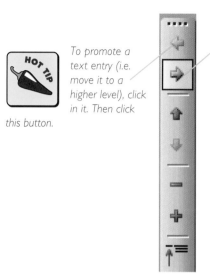

To promote a text entry (i.e. move it to a higher level), click in it. Then click this button.

4 In the Outlining toolbar (View, Toolbars, Outlining), click here to demote the 2nd slide to a sub-entry in the first

5 Type in sub-text and press Enter. Repeat as often as necessary

When you save your presentation to HTML or Single File Web Page format (pages 66 thru 71), the Outline tab becomes a Table of Contents to help you navigate your way thru your slides.

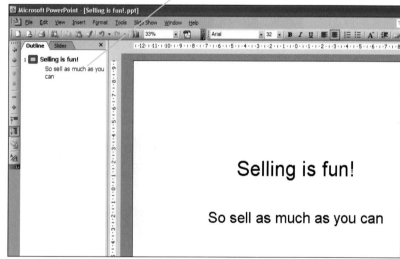

6 When you've finished with the first slide, press Ctrl+Enter to jump to the next. Use the earlier techniques to add text to this. Repeat these procedures as often as necessary

Moving slides

To reposition slides in Outline view, carry out the following steps:

1. Click a slide marker (to select multiple slides, Shift+click)

You can also move demoted entries within slides or to other slides. Triple-click a demoted entry to select it then drag it to a new level within the original slide or to a new one.

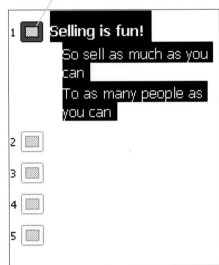

Want to print out your outline? You can do this but you'll have to use Microsoft Word.
First, get the outline the way you want to print it by expanding the relevant entries. Hit File, Send To, Microsoft Office Word. In the dialog, select Outline only and hit OK. Now print it out (Ctrl+P) in the usual way.

2. Drag the slide(s) to a new location in the Outline tree

To adjust an outline entry's indent, hit Alt+ Shift+Right cursor to increase it or Alt+Shift+Left cursor to do the opposite.

3. You can use keyboard shortcuts, too. Alt+ Shift+Up cursor moves the selection up while Alt+Shift+ Down cursor reverses the direction

Select the relevant slides by holding down Shift as you click their markers then click the Summary Slide button in the Outlining toolbar:

PowerPoint now inserts the new slide in front of the 1st selected one.

Hiding/displaying entries

An important feature of PowerPoint 2003's Outline view is the ability to hide or reveal entries. This lets you alternate between a useful overview and viewing entries in detail. Do the following:

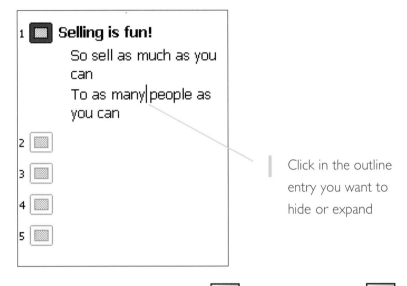

Click in the outline entry you want to hide or expand

2 In the Outlining toolbar, click [—] to hide the entry or [+] to expand it

You can click in Outline text and edit it in the normal way.

3 The underlining denotes that the sub-entries in the example above have now been (temporarily) hidden

Hiding entries is called "collapsing". Expanding is the reverse.

4 Optional – to re-hide or re-expand an entry, repeat step 2 as appropriate. Or double-click its marker

Searching for text

PowerPoint 2003 lets you search for specific text within a slide show. You can also:

- limit the search to words which match the case of the text you specify (e.g. if you search for "Sales", PowerPoint 2003 will not go to slides which contain "sales" or "SALES")

- limit the search to whole words (e.g. if you search for "check", PowerPoint 2003 will not find slides which contain "checks")

Starting a text search

Pull down the Edit menu and click Find. Now do the following:

1 To restrict a find operation to specific text, pre-select it

Unlike other Office programs, PowerPoint does not let you search for wildcards.

2 Hit Ctrl+F

3 Type in the text you want to find

5 Click here to start the search

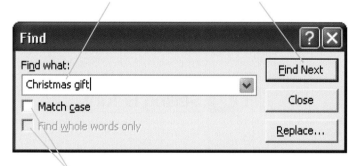

4 Optional – click either or both of these to limit the search

6 Repeat step 5 to locate additional matches

Replacing text

When you've located text, you can have PowerPoint 2003 replace it automatically (or one instance at a time) with any text you choose.

When you undertake a find-and-replace operation, you can (as with find operations) make the search component case-specific, or limit it to whole-word matches.

Initiating a find-and-replace operation

1 To restrict a replace operation to specific text, pre-select it

2 Hit Ctrl+H

3 Type in the text you want to find

4 Type in the replacement text

Before you begin replacing text, specify any parameters you need here.

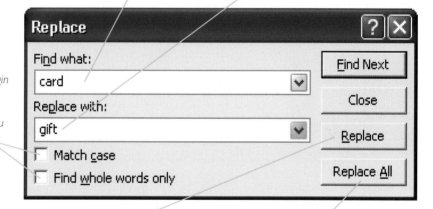

5 Click Replace to replace the 1st instance of the specified text

6 Or click Replace All to replace all instances of the specified text

Spell-checking

PowerPoint 2003 lets you check text in two ways:

- on-the-fly, as you type in text

- separately, after the text has been entered

Checking text on-the-fly

This is the default. When automatic checking is in force, PowerPoint 2003 flags words it doesn't recognize with a wavy red underline. If the word or phrase is wrong, right-click in it. Then carry out steps 1, 2, 3 OR 4:

PowerPoint stores your additions in a special dictionary called CUSTOM.DIC.

Following step 2 ensures that the word is ignored in this checking session only. To ignore it forever, carry out step 3 instead.

1 If an alternative is correct, click it to substitute it for the wrong version

2 Click Ignore All if you want the flagged word to stand

4 If the flagged word is wrong but can't be corrected now, click Spelling and complete the dialog (see the facing page)

3 Click Add to Dictionary to have the word added to your user dictionary

Disabling on-the-fly checking

To keep spell-checking on-the-fly but without the red lines, check "Hide all spelling errors".

1 Pull down the Tools menu and click Options

2 Activate the Spelling and Style tab in the Options dialog, then uncheck "Check spelling as you type"

3 Click OK

To check text in another supported language, select the text then choose Tools, Language. In the Language dialog, select a new language and click OK. Now hit F7 to begin the spell-check.

Checking text separately

PowerPoint 2003 starts spell-checking the presentation from the present location. When it encounters a word or phrase it doesn't recognize, it flags it and produces a special dialog (see below). Usually, it provides alternative suggestions; if one of these is correct, you can opt to have it replace the flagged word. You can do this singly (i.e. just this instance is replaced) or globally (where all future instances – but only within the current checking session – are replaced).

Alternatively, you can have PowerPoint ignore *this* instance of the flagged word, ignore *all* future instances of the word or add the word to CUSTOM.DIC. After this, PowerPoint resumes checking.

1 To check all the text within the active slide show in one go, hit F7

2 If one of the suggestions here is correct, click it, then follow step 3 or 4

If none of the suggestions are correct, type the correct word in the Change to: field then follow step 2 followed by 3 or 4.

5 Click Ignore to ignore just this instance

6 Click Ignore All to ignore all future instances

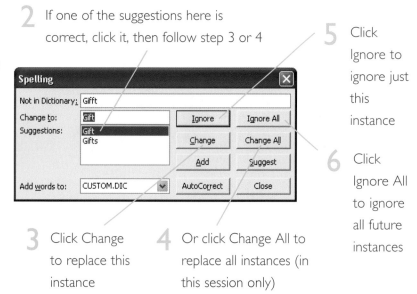

3 Click Change to replace this instance

4 Or click Change All to replace all instances (in this session only)

7 Alternatively, click Add to Dictionary to have the word added to your user dictionary

Searching for synonyms

PowerPoint lets you search for synonyms while you're editing your presentation. You do this by calling up the resident Thesaurus. The Thesaurus categorizes words into meanings; each meaning is allocated various synonyms from which you can choose. The Thesaurus may also supply antonyms. For example, if you look up "good", PowerPoint lists "poor" as an antonym.

Using the Thesaurus

1   Alt+click the word for which you want a synonym or antonym

2   Click here and select Thesaurus: English (U.S.)

If the Thesaurus doesn't function, reinstall it.

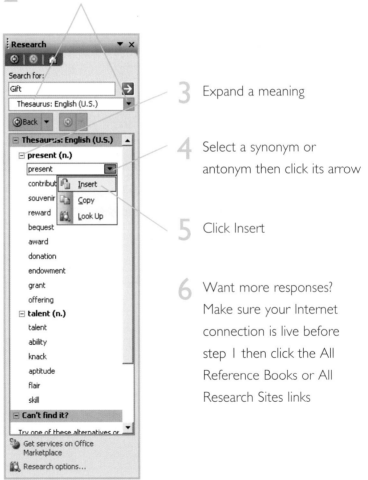

3   Expand a meaning

4   Select a synonym or antonym then click its arrow

5   Click Insert

6   Want more responses? Make sure your Internet connection is live before step 1 then click the All Reference Books or All Research Sites links

Translating text

PowerPoint 2003 has a special Task Pane called Research. As we've just seen on the facing page, this incorporates a Thesaurus. However, it has a lot of other goodies as well, most or all of them online. Use the Research pane to find out all sorts of information. You can also use it to translate text into foreign languages.

Translating text

Be careful how much weight you attach to translation results. For example, "This cake is covered in nuts" translates in Italian as: "Questa torta è coperta in dadi". This is a bit hard to swallow since "dadi" means nuts (as in bolts).

1 With your Internet connection live, Alt+click once

3 Enter the text you want translated

5 Click here

2 Select Translation

4 Select base and target languages

6 The translation appears here

7 Translation no good? Try some of the alternative options here

Carrying out research

We've already seen how the Research pane can be used to translate text. You can do a lot more with it than this, though.

> With your Internet connection live, Alt+click

3 Enter text you want to look up (as a general rule, try entering individual words or phrases and "building up" results)

Microsoft provides a course that you can take to familiarize yourself with PowerPoint's research facilities. Open Office Online then search for this topic: **See what you can do with the Research service.**

4 If PowerPoint doesn't start searching straightaway, click here

2 Select a reference or research facility

5 The reference appears here – expand any likely-looking categories

You can add your own favorite services (including intranet sites) to the Research pane. To do this, click Research options. In the Research Options dialog, check or uncheck services as appropriate. Or hit Add Services then type in the address for the new service(s) you want to add.

6 Haven't found what you want? Try some of the alternative options here

7 Need help with spelling a word? Enter the first few letters in Search for then hit Return. You should see the word you need under "Spelling alternatives"

Saving slide shows

It's important to save your presentation at frequent intervals, in order to avoid data loss in the event of a hardware fault or power interruption.

Saving a presentation for the first time

Hit Ctrl+S

3 Click here. In the drop-down list, click a drive/folder combination

Click any buttons here for access to the relevant folders. For instance, to save files to your Desktop, click Desktop.

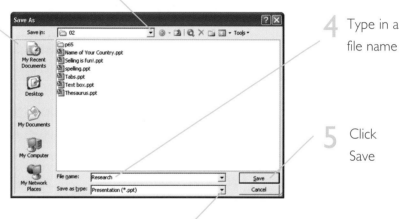

4 Type in a file name

5 Click Save

Re step 2 – to save slide shows to third-party formats or as graphics files, select a format. If a message launches, specify whether you want to save all the slides or just the active one.

(If you export to graphics files, all the slides are saved as separate images in the folder you specify.)

2 Click here. In the list, click the format you want to save to

Saving previously saved presentations

Hit Ctrl+S

2 No dialog launches; instead, PowerPoint 2003 saves the latest version of your slide show to disk, overwriting the previous one

Web publishing – an overview

Preliminaries

You can save presentations – usually in HTML (HyperText Markup Language) format – to network, Web or FTP servers. You can do this if you've created a shortcut to the appropriate folder.

With regard to HTML, the above actions are possible because Microsoft's HTML format has the following qualities:

- it's a Companion File format (Microsoft regards it as occupying the same status as its proprietary formats); this means that you can create *and* share rich Web documents with the same PowerPoint 2003 tools used to create printed documents

- it duplicates the functionality of the proprietary formats (i.e. all the usual PowerPoint 2003 features are preserved when saving in HTML format)

- it's recognized by the Windows Clipboard. This means that data can be copied from Internet Explorer and pasted directly into PowerPoint 2003

Types of Web saving

PowerPoint 2003 lets you work with two main types of Web page:

HTML files

You can publish presentation as standard HTML files in the usual way. These files have all the benefits listed above.

Single File Web Pages (formerly known as Web archives)

Single File Web Pages are special aggregate HTML files which:

- combine and unify all Web site elements (text and pictures)

- can be published or sent via email as just one file

Single File Web Pages have the extension *.mht or *.mhtml and are supported by all versions of Internet Explorer after (and including) 4.0.

Preparing to save to the Internet

You can save presentations (usually in HTML – HyperText Markup Language – format) to network, Web or FTP servers. You can do this so long as you've created a shortcut to the folder that contains them.

To create a shortcut to a Web/FTP folder, you must have a live Internet connection, rights to view/save files and its URL.

To create a shortcut to an Intranet folder, you must have a network connection, rights to view/save files and its network address.

Creating shortcuts to FTP folders

1 Launch the PowerPoint Open or Save As dialog

2 Select Add/Modify FTP Locations

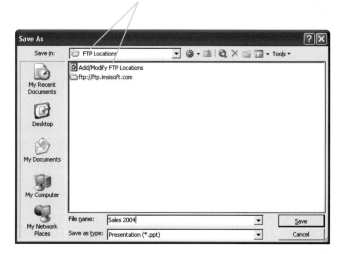

3 Complete the dialog (as here, some FTP sites are Anonymous and don't require a password)

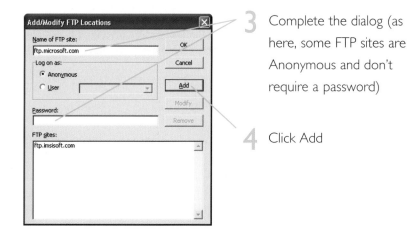

4 Click Add

Creating shortcuts to Web folders

1 Launch the PowerPoint Open or Save As dialog

3 Click here

Creating shortcuts to local network folders may require a different procedure. See your system administrator.

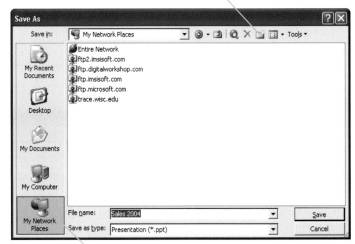

2 Click here

4 Complete the Add Network Place Wizard – basically, you'll need to provide details of the location your new shortcut will open:

Publishing to the Web

Previewing your work before saving

It's a very good idea to preview your presentation before you publish it.

Hit File, Web Page Preview to launch your browser with your presentation displayed in it

Publishing presentations – the quick route

Hit File, Save as Web Page

2 Click here. In the list, select a recipient (see also pages 67 thru 68)

You'd normally use this method to save a copy of all or part of a presentation to your own PC.

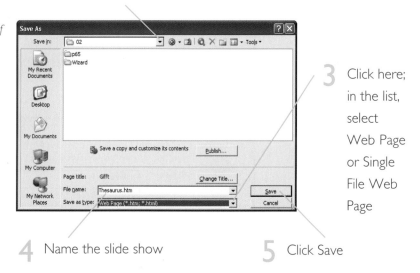

3 Click here; in the list, select Web Page or Single File Web Page

4 Name the slide show

5 Click Save

Publishing presentations – the detailed route

On page 69, we looked at how to save a presentation to the Web with the minimum of preparation. However, you can also use a slightly different route which lets you customize how the slide show is saved. You can:

- specify that the whole presentation is published

- select which slides should be published

- opt to exclude speaker notes

- aim the presentation at specific browsers (or at all browsers – this produces bigger files)

- set detailed Web options

1 Pull down the File menu and click Save as Web Page

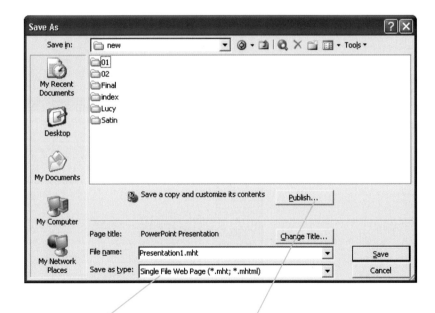

2 Select an output format (Web Page or Single File Web Page)

3 Click Publish

To set Web options (like specifying a target browser, screen resolutions and how fonts are supported), click Web Options. Complete the dialog that launches.

4 Select Complete presentation or specify slides to include

5 Select a browser option

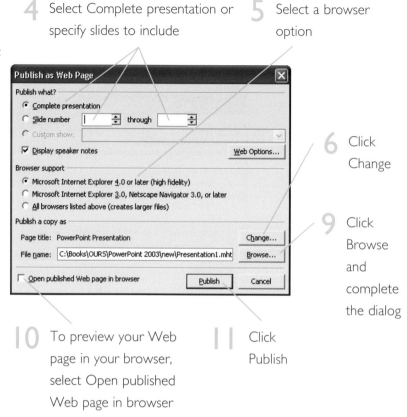

6 Click Change

9 Click Browse and complete the dialog

10 To preview your Web page in your browser, select Open published Web page in browser

11 Click Publish

7 Name the presentation (this appears in the browser's title bar)

If you're using Word 2003, you can send text directly to PowerPoint; when you do this, you create a new presentation (but you'll probably have to edit it fairly extensively).

First, ensure no dialog boxes are open in PowerPoint. Then, in Word, choose File, Send To, Microsoft Office PowerPoint.

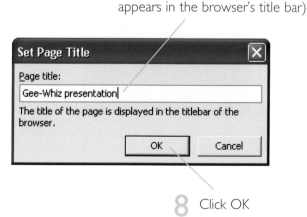

8 Click OK

Opening slide shows

There are lots of ways to open your PowerPoint presentations.

To open a Web- or intranet-based slide show, right-click any toolbar and select Web. In the Web toolbar, click the Go button and select Open Hyperlink in the menu. In the Open Internet Address dialog, type in the presentation's address and name. Click OK.

You can also launch the Open dialog directly by hitting Ctrl+O.

You can use the Open dialog to create a new slide show based on Microsoft Word, RTF or text files:

Word and RTF files   *The outline is structured hierarchically by heading styles*

Text files   *The outline is structured by tabs*

In the Files of type: field, select All Outlines... Double-click the file you want to base the new presentation on. (You'll almost certainly need to revise the new slide show.)

1 If the Task Pane isn't visible, hit Ctrl+F1

2 If your Task Pane doesn't look like this, click the arrow and select Getting Started

3 Click an existing presentation to open it

4 If the presentation you want to open isn't listed, click More . . .

5 Use the Open dialog to:

- select a file type (you can also open slide shows in third-party formats)

- locate and double-click the presentation you want to open

Packaging presentations

You can copy your presentations to CD then send them to people who don't have PowerPoint installed (yes, there are still a few out there) and have them run it. You can do this because of a special PowerPoint viewer that is automatically packaged with your presentation.

1 Make sure the copy of the presentation you want to package no longer contains inappropriate information (this includes comments and annotations)

If you don't have Windows XP or later installed, you can't package directly to CD.
You can however package your presentation to a folder on your hard drive and then copy it to CD via CD burning software.

2 If you don't want the packaged presentation to be password-protected, remove the protection before you begin the packaging process

3 Hit File, Package for CD

4 Name the packaged presentation

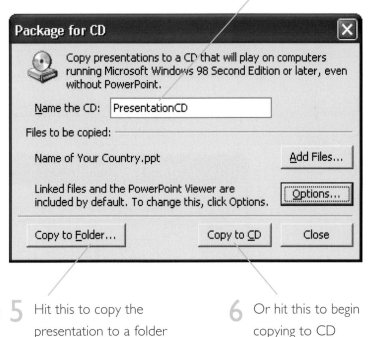

Package for CD

Copy presentations to a CD that will play on computers running Microsoft Windows 98 Second Edition or later, even without PowerPoint.

Name the CD: PresentationCD

Files to be copied:

Name of Your Country.ppt   Add Files...

Linked files and the PowerPoint Viewer are included by default. To change this, click Options.   Options...

Copy to Folder...   Copy to CD   Close

If you know the person you want to send your presentation to definitely has PowerPoint 2003, you can exclude the PowerPoint viewer from the package. Hit Options then uncheck PowerPoint Viewer...

(You can also use the Options dialog to customize how the package plays – for example, you can disable Autostart. Just click in the box under PowerPoint Viewer... and select an option.)

5 Hit this to copy the presentation to a folder or network location

6 Or hit this to begin copying to CD

7   If you carried out step 5 on page 73, specify a name and address for the new folder you want to package your presentation to then hit OK

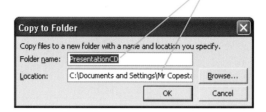

8   If you carried out step 6 on page 73, follow the onscreen instructions (and then complete steps 9 thru 11)

9   When you've inserted a blank CD, copying begins:

10   When copying is complete, hit Yes or No

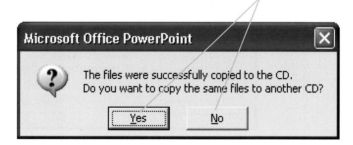

11   To run your presentation, the recipient simply inserts the CD. The PowerPoint Viewer autostarts automatically and runs your presentation

Designing your slides

Now it's time to fine-tune the appearance of your slides. Masters (a bit like styles in Word 2003) ensure your slides have consistent formatting and you can also use them to insert objects (like logos) on all of them. You'll add new masters by applying design templates then do master housekeeping. You'll also apply another aspect of design templates – color schemes – as another way of making sure your slides are consistent. Color schemes are great but you're not restricted to the basic ones: you can easily create your own. You can also copy color schemes between presentations with Format Painter and change the background of individual slides. You can even apply pictures as backgrounds.

Covers

Chapter Three

Customizing slides – an overview

You can also enhance the appearance of handouts and notes by using the Handout and Notes masters – see Chapter 7.

You can use these techniques to enhance slide appearance quickly and conveniently. You can:

*   customize Slide masters

*   customize Title masters

*   apply a new color scheme

*   apply design templates

Slide masters are aspects of the overriding design template. They control text placing/formatting but not content. Thus you can amend the appearance or position of text but not the text itself.

If you have specific text you want to appear on all slides apart from the first, insert a text box into the Slide master. Insert one into the Title master to impact just the first slide.

Slide masters

Slide masters are control slides which determine the format and position of all titles and text on slides (but see the tip on the immediate left). You can also insert other objects – e.g. pictures – onto a Slide master; when you do this, they're reproduced (unless you change this) on all slides after the first. In this way, if you want a picture – for instance, a company logo – to appear on every slide except the first, you can simply insert it on the Slide master.

In this way, masters are like word processor styles: changes to the master automatically ripple through the rest of the slide show.

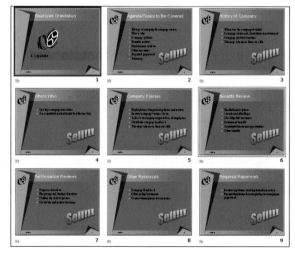

(a Wordart object – see page 104) has been added to the master and appears on every slide but the first

More specifically, use Title masters to amend slides that have had the Title Slide layout (the first layout in the Slide Layout Task Pane) applied. You typically would use Title masters to start new sections in your presentation.

Title masters

Title masters perform the same function as Slide masters, but only in respect of the Title (first) slide.

Color schemes

Color schemes are integrated collections of colors which are guaranteed to complement each other. Each color scheme contains eight balanced colors which are automatically applied to slide elements such as text, backgrounds and fills.

Color schemes are tailor-made for the design template which hosts them.

You can apply color schemes to individual slides, or to the whole of a presentation. Even better, you can also create and use your own color schemes.

Design templates

Design templates – otherwise known simply as designs – are collections of:

If you plan to work on both the Slide and Title masters, work on the Slide master first (because text formatting changes on the Slide master are automatically mirrored in the Title master).

- Slide masters (and often Title masters)

- color schemes

- specific fonts which complement other elements in the relevant design

When you add a new design template, you automatically insert a new master. For this reason, if you want to implement a presentation-wide change, you'll need to change each master (or master pair, if you're also using the title master).

When you apply a design template to a slide show (or to specific slides within it), any objects you've already applied to the Slide master (e.g. pictures or text boxes) remain. Also, the template takes precedence over the existing Slide master, Title master and color scheme. This means that when you create new slides, they automatically assume the characteristics of the new design template, irrespective of any layouts you may have applied previously (see page 39 for how to use layouts).

Summary

Title masters share some styles (formatting features) in common with slide masters.

Appropriate editing of Slide/Title masters (or the application of a new color scheme) represents a convenient technique for ensuring your slide show has a uniform appearance and/or content. Applying a new design template is a way of doing both at the same time.

Working with masters

Editing masters is easy and convenient.

Launching masters

Pull down the View menu and do the following:

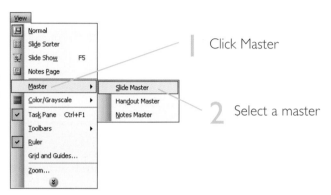

Click Master

See Chapter 7 for how to launch the Handout and Notes masters.

Select a master

Editing masters

You can use the techniques shown here in any master.

Click in a text entry, then apply any appropriate formatting enhancements

For how to insert pictures into master slides, see Chapter 6.

For how to work with headers/ footers, see pages 89 thru 90.

Click in a specialized text box, then apply any appropriate formatting enhancements

Adding new masters

PowerPoint 2003 is set up to permit multiple masters. If you don't want this, choose Tools, Options. In the Options dialog, select the Edit tab. Check Multiple Masters in the Disable new features section. Click OK.

You can replace existing masters with new ones from design templates. Alternatively, you can simply add new ones.

Replacing/inserting new masters

1 Hit View, Master, Slide Master

2 Optional – to replace specific masters, select one or more

Another way to insert a new Slide master is to click this button in the dedicated Slide Master View toolbar:

Or click this button for a Title Slide master:

3 Hit Format, Slide Design

4 Right-click a design then specify how it should be applied

Masters come in pairs: the Slide and the Title Master. PowerPoint makes it clear they're linked by attaching a link symbol:

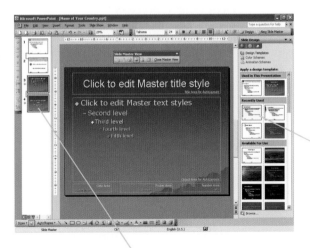

Designs used in this presentation display in the Recently Used section of the Task Pane

5 Here, an additional slide-title master pair has been inserted because Add Design was selected in step 4

Master housekeeping

You can perform various actions on masters.

Renaming masters

If you go to master view but don't see a master, you'll have to add one – see page 79.

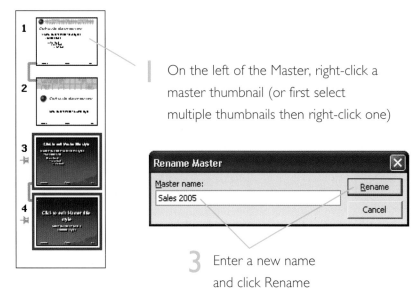

On the left of the Master, right-click a master thumbnail (or first select multiple thumbnails then right-click one)

3 Enter a new name and click Rename

2 In the menu, click Rename Master

Protecting masters

When you protect a master, PowerPoint inserts this symbol to the left of its thumbnail:

To prevent a master from being automatically deleted (e.g. when all associated slides are deleted), follow step 1 above

2 In the menu, click Preserve Master

Deleting masters
You can only delete masters you've added, not the default masters.

Follow step 1 above

2 In the menu, click Delete Master – deletion is immediate (but can be undone, if necessary)

Restoring masters

Within any master, you can restore elements/placeholders you've previously deleted.

You can also use Undo to restore elements.

| Pull down the Format menu and do one of the following:

- click Master Layout (for Slide and Title masters)
- click Handout Master Layout (for Handout masters), or;
- click Notes Master Layout (for Notes masters)

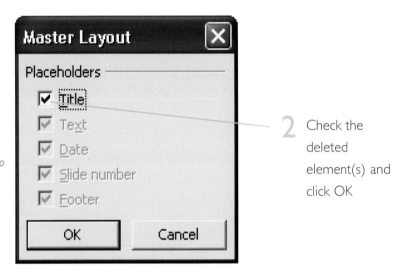

2 Check the deleted element(s) and click OK

Having multiple masters is very useful but remember that, when you need to add an item to all your slides, you'll probably have to add it to more than one master.

Duplicating masters

Sometimes, it's a lot easier to copy an existing (and complex) master and then edit it than to create a new master from scratch.

| Left-click one master (or Ctrl+click multiple masters)

2 Hit Insert, Duplicate Slide Master

Applying color schemes

Any PowerPoint 2003 presentation automatically has various color schemes available to it – they're contained in the design template associated with the slide show. Design templates can have up to 16 color schemes, each consisting of 8 harmonized colors.

Applying a new color scheme is a quick and effective way to give a presentation a new and consistent look. Making slight but telling changes to existing schemes is also useful. For example, you might want to adapt a presentation's colors to fit a specific show or event... PowerPoint 2003 lets you do this very easily and conveniently.

The really fun part comes in when you tweak a color scheme's colors to match the theme of an outside event like a convention – see page 84. (When you amend a color scheme, what you get in effect is a new scheme.)

Another plus is the fact that when you apply colors independently of color schemes (for example, when you recolor text via the Font dialog), the new colors are automatically made available in color dialogs in a way which makes it clear they're distinct from color scheme colors. This makes it very easy to maintain color consistency:

Here, a non-standard color has been applied to text. As a result, launching the Color fly-out in the Font dialog produces this result:

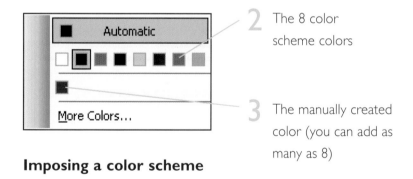

2 The 8 color scheme colors

3 The manually created color (you can add as many as 8)

Imposing a color scheme

To restrict the color scheme to one or more slides, do one of the following:

- In Normal view, go to the slide whose color scheme you want to replace

- In Slide Sorter view, select one or more slides

2 Hit Format, Slide Design

To add a new color scheme to notes or handouts, hit View, Master, Handout Master or View, Notes Page just before step 3.

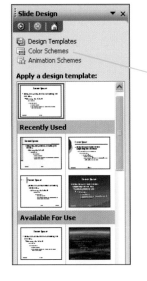

3 Click Color Schemes

Some design templates have more color schemes associated with them than others.

When you change the colors in a color scheme, PowerPoint creates a new scheme and adds it to this version of the Task Pane.

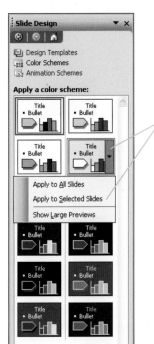

4 Click on the right of a color scheme, then specify how it should be applied

Changing colors in a scheme

You can change individual colors within a color scheme. When you do this, all associated slide objects are automatically updated.

Amending a scheme color

 Colors in color schemes resemble word processor graphics styles.

1 To restrict the changes to one or more slides, do one of the following:

- In Normal view, go to the slide whose color scheme you want to amend

- In Slide Sorter view, select one or more slides

2 Launch the Color Schemes version of the Slide Design Task Pane (see page 83) then hit the Edit Color Schemes link

 To delete a color scheme, select the Standard tab. Select a scheme and click Delete Scheme. (You can't, however, delete a slide show's one remaining color scheme.)

3 Select Custom

4 Select a slide component, then Change Color

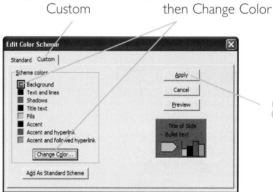

8 Click Apply

 *To ensure that the color changes you've made are saved with the presentation, click the Add As Standard Scheme button.*

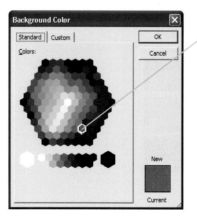

5 Select the Standard tab then a color

6 Or select the Custom tab then drag out a new color

7 Either way, hit OK

Format Painter

You can use Format Painter to copy formatting between text. Format Painter can also copy any formatting you've applied to a picture (e.g. a border) to another image.

You can use a shortcut (the Format Painter) to copy a color scheme from one presentation to one or more slides in another.

Copying color schemes

1 With both presentations open in Normal view, pull down the Window menu and click Arrange All

2 Carry out step 3 below. In step 4, single-click for one copy or double-click for multiple copies (and see the HOT TIP)

To copy the formatting to more than one slide, double-click in step 4. In step 5, click as many icons as required. When you've finished, press Esc.

4 In the Standard toolbar, click or double-click the Format Painter icon:

3 Click the icon for the slide whose scheme you want to copy

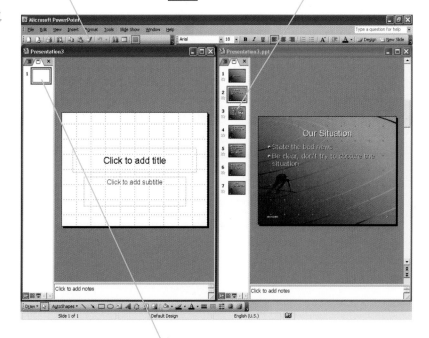

5 Click the icon representing the slide you want to format

6 The new color scheme is now available in the target presentation's Slide Design Task Pane

Applying design templates

The AutoContent wizard uses a specialized form of design template called the content template.

When you apply a new design template to a presentation, you impose a potent combination of masters and color schemes. For this reason, designs often represent the best and most convenient way to give presentations an effective and consistent appearance.

Imposing a design

1 To restrict the changes to one or more slides, do one of the following:

The Slide Design Task Pane defaults to the folder which holds PowerPoint 2003 templates. If you want to use a template stored in a different drive/folder combination, select Browse at the base of the Task Pane and select it in the Apply Design Template dialog.

- In Normal view, go to the slide you want to re-design
- In Slide Sorter view, select one or more slides

2 Pull down the Format menu and click Slide Design

3 Click on the right of a design template

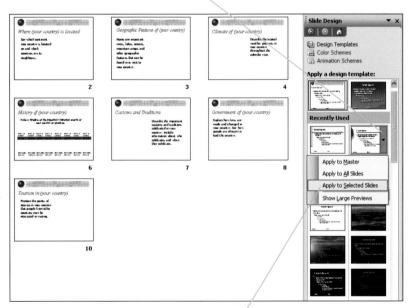

You can also use slide shows, HTML files or Single File Web Pages as the basis for a design.

Launch the Apply Design Template dialog (see the above tip.) In the dialog box, click in the Files of type: field and select the appropriate format. Double-click the file you want to use.

To have design templates display more clearly, right-click one in the Task Pane. In the menu, select Show Large Previews.

4 Specify the extent of the change

Applying new backgrounds

You can also apply new backgrounds to slides, as a separate action.

Change a slide's background if you don't want to use all the elements in a design template – for example, you might just want to insert a simple color or fill.

Imposing a background

1 To restrict the changes to one or more slides, do one of the following:

- In Normal view, go to the slide you want to affect
- In Slide Sorter view, select one or more slides

2 Pull down the Format menu and click Background

Make sure "Omit background graphics from master" isn't checked if you want to view items you've inserted into your master slides.

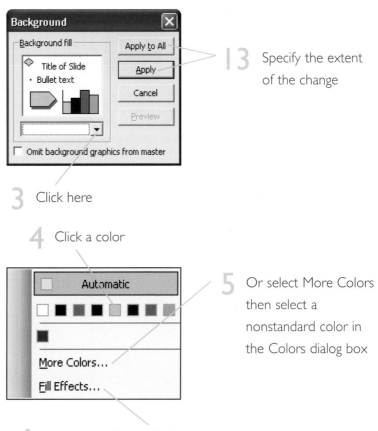

13 Specify the extent of the change

3 Click here

4 Click a color

5 Or select More Colors then select a nonstandard color in the Colors dialog box

6 To apply a fill, hit Fill Effects then see overleaf

7 Select Gradient, Texture or Pattern, according to the type of fill you want to insert

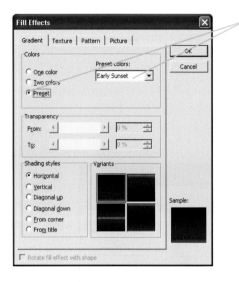

8 Complete the dialog – for example, if you want a gradient (graduated) fill, it's a good idea to select Preset then apply a preset fill

9 You can even apply pictures as backgrounds! To do this, select the Picture tab instead

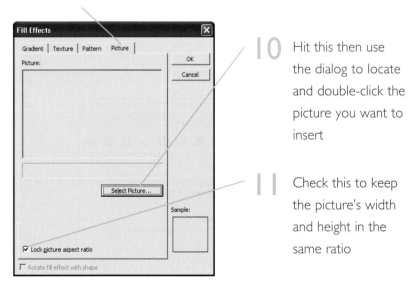

10 Hit this then use the dialog to locate and double-click the picture you want to insert

11 Check this to keep the picture's width and height in the same ratio

12 Either way, click OK

Working with headers/footers

Headers are text elements which appear at the top of handouts or notes; footers are elements which appear at the base of slides, handouts or notes.

Typically, you'll use headers and footers to display:

- the date and time of the presentation

- the slide or page number

- information specific to the current presentation

Once you've inserted information in headers and/or footers, you can change their appearance or position.

Using footers in slides

You don't have to use headers and footers in your slide shows. For instance, it might be helpful to disable them in slides but leave them in force in notes and handouts.

1 To restrict the changes to one or more slides, do one of the following:

- In Normal view, go to the slide whose footer scheme you want to amend

- In Slide Sorter view, select one or more slides

To move or reformat header and footer elements, launch the appropriate master. Select the element(s). Then do either or both of the following:

- *drag them to a new location*
- *apply new formatting characteristics*

2 Hit View, Header and Footer

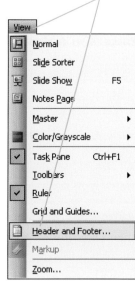

To add the date/ time or slide number anywhere on a slide, click inside the relevant text placeholder or text box. Choose Insert, Slide Number or Insert, Date and Time.

3 Ensure the Slide tab is active

8 Click Apply to All to impact all slides

Select Update automatically to insert the date and time routinely, or Fixed then type in your own format.

To amend the number at which numbering begins, choose File, Page Setup. In the Number slides from: field, type in a new start point.

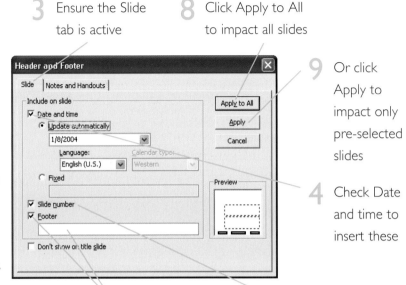

9 Or click Apply to impact only pre-selected slides

4 Check Date and time to insert these

5 To amplify the footer, check Footer and insert extra data

6 To insert the slide number check Slide number

7 To remove footers from title slides, check "Don't show on title slide". (To disable footers in all other slides, uncheck the appropriate fields)

Using headers/footers in notes and handouts

1 Launch the Header and Footer dialog box but this time select the Notes and Handouts tab

2 Complete the dialog as above with these exceptions:

- Check the Page number field if you want to insert the handout/notes page number on each page

- Check Header if you want to add supplementary header content, then enter the content in the field below

Inserting lines, curves and shapes

Now is a great time to create and insert "objects" (simple or complex graphics) in order to make your presentations even more visually effective. You'll create lines, arrows, curves, rectangles, squares, ellipses and circles. If this isn't enough, you can also insert AutoShapes (extraordinarily flexible graphics that are very easy to use) including special lines called "connectors" that you can use to link objects, so when you move them they'll stay together. Check out the WordArt section, too, for some fancy text that can really make slides stand out.

Covers

Chapter Four

Creating lines

By adding a variety of objects (lines, curves and special shapes called AutoShapes) you can make your presentations a lot more visual and therefore more effective.

Creating a straight line

You can create lots of different types of lines: straight lines, single- or double-arrowed lines, curved lines and freeform lines.

1 In Normal or Notes Page view (View, Normal or View, Notes Page), refer to the Drawing toolbar (View, Toolbars, Drawing) and do the following:

2 Click here

You can create lines called connectors that "stick" to shapes. When you move the shapes, the connectors move with them. Neat, huh?

Click AutoShapes in the Drawing toolbar. Select Connectors then a connector. Move the pointer over the object you want to attach the connector to and click a connection site (a blue circle). Find another site in a second object and click it. (Attached connectors show as red circles; unattached ones are green.)

3 Drag to define the line. To constrain the line to 15° increments, hold down Shift; to define the line outwards (to the left and right) from the starting point, hold down Ctrl

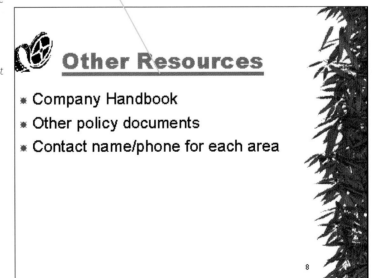

To create a double-arrowed line, you should click the following icon instead:

Creating a single-arrowed line

1 In Normal or Notes Page view (View, Normal or View, Notes Page), refer to the Drawing toolbar (View, Toolbars, Drawing) and do the following:

2 Click here

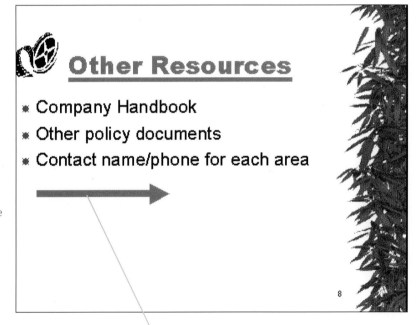

The lines in these examples have been thickened. To thicken a line (or other object), select it. Refer to the Drawing toolbar and click this icon:

In the graphic list, select a line weight. (Or click More Lines and use the Colors and Lines section of the Format AutoShape dialog to customize a line.)

3 Drag to define the line. To constrain the line to 15° increments, hold down Shift; to define the line outwards (to the left and right) from the starting point, hold down Ctrl

Creating rectangles

Drawing a rectangle

1 In Normal or Notes Page view (View, Normal or View, Notes Page), refer to the Drawing toolbar (View, Toolbars, Drawing) and do the following:

2 Click here

3 Drag to define the rectangle (to draw a square, hold down Shift)

To apply fills to objects, follow the techniques described on page 101.

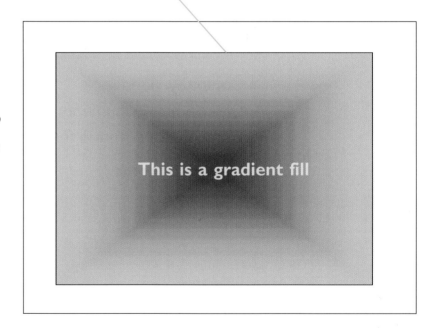

This is a gradient fill

4 You can use another route to create a rectangle. Just click in your slide where you want the object to begin. PowerPoint 2003 inserts the following (with or without the fill):

5 Resize the new object

Creating ellipses

Drawing an ellipse

1 In Normal or Notes Page view (View, Normal or View, Notes Page), refer to the Drawing toolbar (View, Toolbars, Drawing) and do the following:

2 Click here

3 Drag to define the rectangle (to draw a circle, hold down Shift)

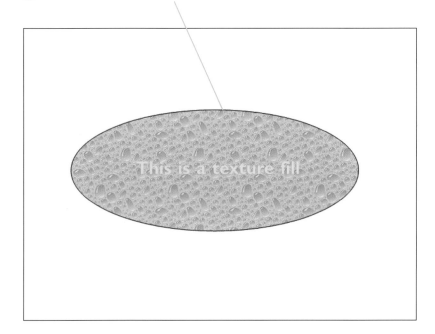

This is a texture fill

4 You can use another route to create a ellipse. Just click in your slide where you want the object to begin. PowerPoint 2003 inserts the following (with or without the fill):

5 Resize the new object

Creating Bézier curves

PowerPoint 2003 lets you create three types of curves. The curves are:

Bézier   Great control and accuracy

Freeform   Freehand curve/line combinations without jagged edges – see page 98

Scribble   A lifelike imitation of freehand drawing – see page 99

Defining Bézier curves

If you need to create curves, you'll normally use this technique. In effect, you tell PowerPoint where 2 or more points should be placed and it creates the appropriate curve(s) between them.

1   Ensure you're using Normal or Notes Pages view. Refer to the Drawing toolbar and click AutoShapes. Select Lines. Click this icon in the fly-out menu:

2   Place the mouse pointer where you want the curve to begin

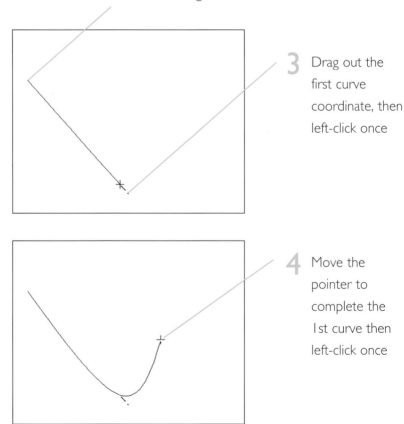

3   Drag out the first curve coordinate, then left-click once

4   Move the pointer to complete the 1st curve then left-click once

5 Optional – move the mouse pointer to define another curve, then left-click

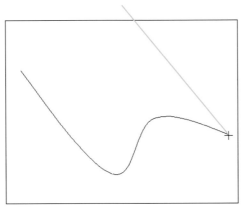

6 Repeat step 5 as often as required

7 When you've finished defining curves, double-click once

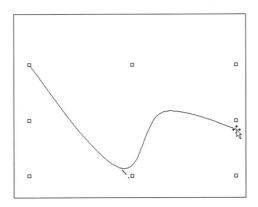

8 Use a different procedure if you want to produce a closed shape like this:

9 Simply left-click once near the curve start point

Creating freeform curves/lines

Using the Freeform tool

Use the Freeform tool to create objects with both curved and straight

components.

1 Ensure you're using Normal or Notes Pages view. Refer to the Drawing toolbar and click AutoShapes. Select Lines. Click this icon in the fly-out menu:

2 Drag to create a freehand shape

3 Or, to create a straight line, left-click then move the mouse pointer and left-click again

4 When you've finished drawing, double-click once

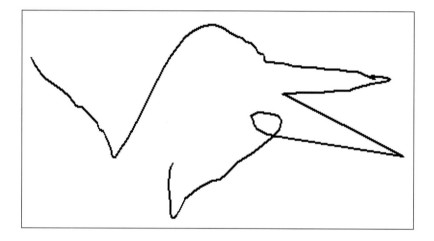

5 Use a different procedure if you want to produce a closed shape like this:

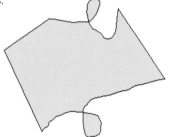

6 Simply left-click once near the object start point

Creating curves with Scribble

Use the Scribble tool to create objects which look as if they were drawn with a pen.

Using the Scribble tool

1 Ensure you're using Normal or Notes Pages view. Refer to the Drawing toolbar and click AutoShapes. Select Lines. Click this icon in the fly-out menu:

2 Drag to create a curve

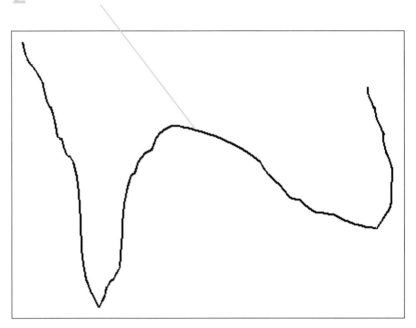

3 Use a different procedure if you want to produce a closed shape like this:

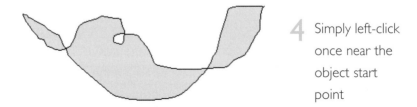

4 Simply left-click once near the object start point

Creating AutoShapes

AutoShapes are an extraordinarily flexible and easy-to-use way to insert a wide variety of shapes into your presentations.

Inserting an AutoShape

1 Ensure you're using Normal or Notes Pages view. Refer to the Drawing toolbar and click AutoShapes

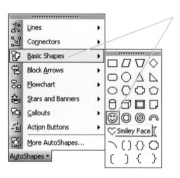

2 Select a category then a specific AutoShape

3 Drag out the shape

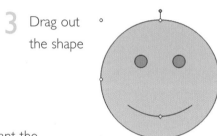

4 Or just click where you want the AutoShape inserted then resize it in the normal way

Rotating AutoShapes

1 Select the AutoShape

2 Click Draw in the Drawing toolbar. In the menu, select Rotate or Flip, Free Rotate

3 All the shape's handles become Rotate handles; drag one to rotate the object

4 Alternatively, just select the AutoShape then drag here

5 To rotate by 90°, click the Draw button. In the menu, click Rotate or Flip. In the submenu, click Rotate Left or Rotate Right.

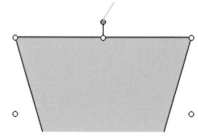

Filling and reshaping AutoShapes

Coloring AutoShapes

Ensure you're using Normal or Notes Pages view. Select the AutoShape then refer to the Drawing toolbar and click the arrow next to this icon:

In addition to the techniques discussed on pages 100 thru 103, you can also use a dialog route to edit shapes. This is especially useful for editing more than one shape at a time.

Double-click any shape (or multiple selected shapes) to produce the Format AutoShape dialog. Activate the appropriate tab, then make the necessary amendments. For example, to amend the object's size, click the Size tab and enter new settings in the Height/Width fields.

2 Select a color (or hit More Fill Colors and use the Colors dialog to select another in the usual way)

3 To apply a special fill, click Fill Effects and complete the Fill Effects dialog in the usual way

Reshaping AutoShapes

To have an AutoShape (or text box) resize to fit the text it contains, double-click the AutoShape or text box frame. In the dialog, select the Text Box tab and tick "Resize AutoShape to fit text". Click OK.

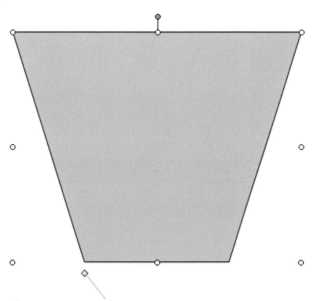

Changes you make to an AutoShape also affect any inserted text.

A lot of AutoShapes have a special yellow handle – drag this to change the AutoShape's shape (but not its size)

Shadowing AutoShapes

You can use these techniques (and those on the facing page) with any drawing object created in PowerPoint.

Ensure you're using Normal or Notes Pages view. Select the AutoShape then refer to the Drawing toolbar and do the following:

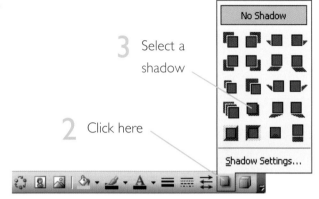

3 Select a shadow

2 Click here

Fine-tuning shadows

It's often a good idea to tweak the shadow PowerPoint gives you, to make it more effective.

Select the AutoShape then hit Shadow Settings in the above fly-out

Click one of these to vary the shadow position. Repeat this as often as required for the full effect

3 To vary the shadow color, click here and select a color in the fly-out

4 Alternatively, select More Shadow Colors in the fly-out and select a new color in the usual way

Converting AutoShapes

Making AutoShapes 3D

Ensure you're using Normal or Notes Pages view. Select the
AutoShape then refer to the Drawing toolbar and do the
following:

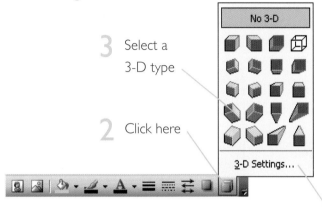

3 Select a
3-D type

2 Click here

4 Click here and use the 3-D Settings toolbar to vary 3-D
settings such as tilt, depth, direction, lighting and color

*If you insert lots
of AutoShapes,
you may have to
set the "order" i.e.
tell PowerPoint
which should be on top. Select
one or more shapes then hit
Draw on the Drawing toolbar.
Select Order followed by an
instruction such as Bring to Front
or Send to Back.*

Converting AutoShapes from one type to another

Ensure you're using Normal or Notes Pages view then select the
AutoShape

2 Click Draw in the Drawing toolbar

3 Select Change AutoShape

4 Select a new category/AutoShape combination in the menus

Using WordArt

In Normal or Notes Page view, you can embellish your slides with WordArt objects. These are text objects with professional-quality, ready-made formatting attributes. WordArt text can add a lot of pizazz to slides.

Don't make the mistake of inserting a lot of WordArt objects on the same slide: using too many spoils the effect.

Adding a WordArt object

Refer to the Drawing toolbar and click this icon:

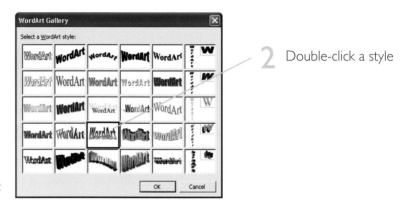

To change a WordArt object's textual content, double-click it. In the Edit WordArt Text dialog, overwrite the selected text and click OK.

2 Double-click a style

3 Specify a font and type size etc.

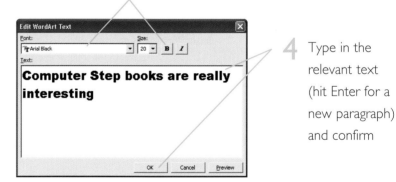

4 Type in the relevant text (hit Enter for a new paragraph) and confirm

Saving WordArt Objects

Right-click the WordArt object and choose Save as Picture

2 Complete the Save As Picture dialog in the normal way

The art of charts

Charts dramatically improve slide impact. They're easy to use, too. You just enter data into a small dedicated window called the Datasheet (it's like a mini version of a standard spreadsheet) and PowerPoint's native charting program – Microsoft Graph – converts it into a chart for you. You can even use Graph in other programs. Once you've gotten your data into a chart in PowerPoint, you're not restricted to the chart type you chose: you can easily convert it into another one. You can format the chart, too, so it has the maximum effect.

You can also import data from other programs (for example, Microsoft Excel 2003) and convert it directly into a chart.

Covers

Chapter Five

Charts – an overview

PowerPoint 2003 makes it easy to insert charts into your presentations. You can do this in two ways:

- by double-clicking chart placeholders (if the slide you're inserting the chart into has had an appropriate layout applied to it)

When you create or work with charts in PowerPoint 2003, you're actually running a separate program called Microsoft Graph. Graph runs seamlessly within the PowerPoint 2003 environment. However, its menus are not personalized i.e. entries aren't promoted or demoted according to frequency of use.

- by using a menu route

When you insert a chart, the data on which it's based is displayed in a special window called the Datasheet. The Datasheet can be regarded as a mini version of a spreadsheet like Microsoft Excel, and contains sample data which you can easily amend.

Once you've inserted a chart, you can:

- edit the data

- reformat the Datasheet

- import data from a variety of external sources, including Microsoft Excel and Lotus 1-2-3 files

- apply a new chart type/sub-type

You can also use Graph to insert charts into other programs (e.g. Word 2003).

In the program, pull down the Insert menu and click Object (this command sometimes varies with the program concerned). Select the Create New tab and double-click Microsoft Graph Chart. Now customize/edit it in the usual way.

- reformat chart objects

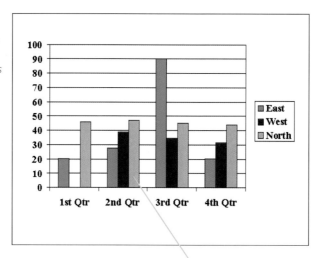

An inserted chart, with sample data

Chart components

PowerPoint 2003 offers 14 overall chart types. There are also numerous sub-types (variants on a theme). In addition, PowerPoint 2003 charts are very customizable: they can contain a wide variety of features/components. The illustration below shows the main ones:

Most charts do not contain all of these elements (they would simply become too cluttered); they're shown here for illustration purposes.

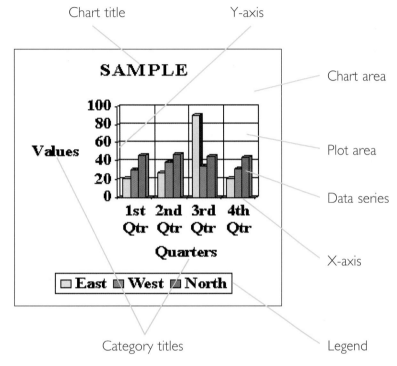

Chart title   Y-axis

Chart area

Plot area

Data series

X-axis

Category titles   Legend

You can animate charts. Select a chart then hit Slide Show, Custom Animation. In the Custom Animation Task Pane, hit the Add Effect button. Select an animation category and then an animation.

Terminology...

A data series is a group of related values taken from a Datasheet row (horizontal) or column (vertical). In this chart, there are three: East, West and North. (For more information on the use of the Datasheet, see pages 109 thru 110.)

These distinctions between the X, Y and Z axes are sometimes blurred.

Axes are lines which border the chart area; chart values are measured against axes. In most charts, the Y (Value) axis is vertical, while the X (Category) axis is horizontal.

Some charts also have a Z (Time) axis that allows values to be related to time.

Inserting charts

The placeholder route

In Normal view, display the slide into which you want to insert the chart. Carry out the following steps:

Double-click a Chart placeholder

Click icon to add content

2 Complete the Datasheet (see the facing page) then click anywhere in the slide

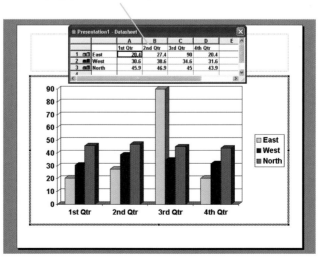

Editing chart data

After you've created a chart, and irrespective of the way you created it, you should revise the data on which it's based.

Amending data

Cells are formed where rows and columns intersect.

To select all cells, click the Select All button:

To select an entire row in the Datasheet, click its row heading; to select a whole column, click its column heading.

1 Right-click the chart and hit Chart Object, Edit then refer to the Datasheet window:

2 Amend the axis titles

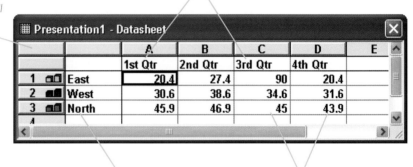

3 Amend the data series titles

4 Amend the chart values, as appropriate

To add gridlines to a chart, select it. Choose Chart, Chart Options. In the dialog, select the Gridlines tab and tick the relevant entries. Click OK.

5 When you've finished, click outside the Datasheet

6 To add a legend to a chart, select it then pull down the Chart menu and click Chart Options

7 In the dialog, select the Legend tab and tick Show legend. Select a placement (e.g. Bottom) and click OK

8 To add a chart title and/or axis titles to a chart, refer to the above dialog, select the Titles tab and type in the relevant titles. Click OK

9 To view or hide the Datasheet, hit View, Datasheet

Reformatting the Datasheet

Formatting changes you make to the Datasheet have no effect on the way your data is represented in the chart, but they can make it easier to edit your data effectively.

To a limited extent, you can customize how the Datasheet presents information. For instance, you can change the typeface/type size and specify how many decimal places numbers use.

Applying a typeface/type size

1 With the Datasheet visible, hit Format, Font

2 Select a new font

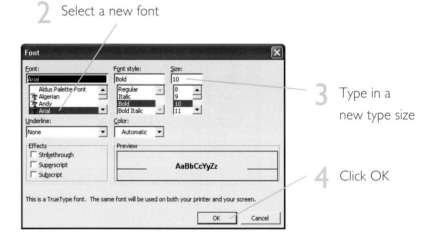

3 Type in a new type size

4 Click OK

Applying a number format

1 In the Datasheet, select the cells you want to amend then hit Format, Number

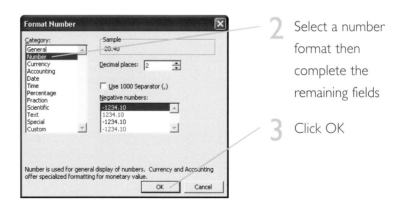

2 Select a number format then complete the remaining fields

3 Click OK

Importing data from Excel

It's often useful to have PowerPoint 2003 create charts from third-party data. You can import:

- Excel files (Excel menus are incorporated into PowerPoint's)

- Lotus 1-2-3 files

- text files, also known as "delimited" or CSV (Comma Separated Value) files

Importing Excel data

1 In Normal view, go to the slide in which you want the new chart created then hit Insert, Chart; PowerPoint 2003 inserts a new chart with sample data and launches the Datasheet

2 If you want the inserted data to begin in any cell other than the upper left, click it

3 Hit Edit, Import File

5 Locate then double-click the file you want to import

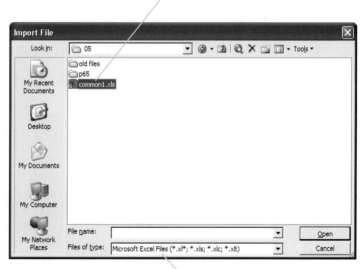

4 Click here; select Microsoft Excel Files... in the list

6 Select an Excel worksheet

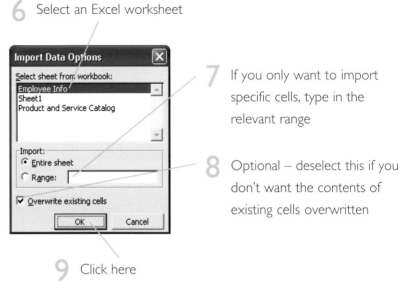

7 If you only want to import specific cells, type in the relevant range

8 Optional – deselect this if you don't want the contents of existing cells overwritten

9 Click here

10 PowerPoint 2003 now creates a new chart based on the imported data

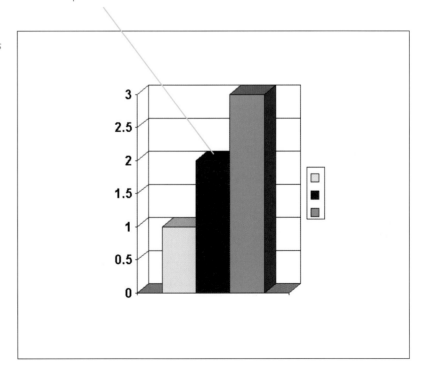

Importing data from text files

1 Launch the Import File dialog (see page 111) but select "Text Files ..." as the import type. Locate then double-click the text file you want to import

2 Optional – select another file type

Importing text files can sometimes be tricky. Complete each stage in the Wizard in line with the instructions. Luckily, however, PowerPoint auto-completes most of the settings and these likely will be right. Only change the defaults if you're certain they're not suitable.

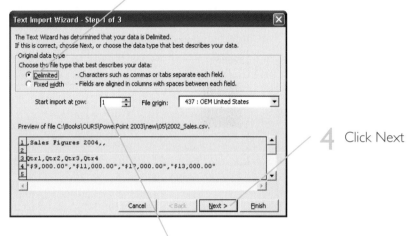

4 Click Next

3 Optional – specify the row where the import should begin

5 Optional – specify a different delimiter

You know when you've picked the right delimiter: at this stage – but not earlier – you can no longer see it in the Data preview section (and the data is properly formatted).

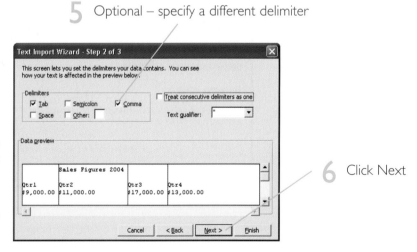

6 Click Next

Repeat steps 7 thru 8 for as many columns as you need to amend.

8 Optional – select a data format

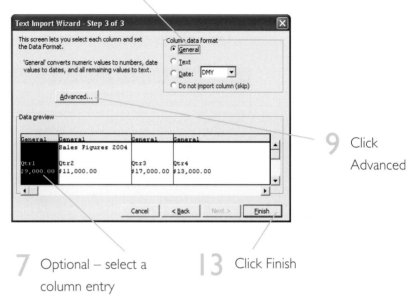

9 Click Advanced

7 Optional – select a column entry

13 Click Finish

HOT TIP

You need to select a separator which is identical to the decimal separator used in the original text file i.e. if the separator is a comma, choose the same. If in doubt, accept the default.

10 Click here; select a decimal separator

11 Click here; select a thousand separator

12 Click here

Applying a new chart type

After you've inserted a chart, you can change the chart type. There are fourteen chart types. Some of the most commonly used are described below. All of the fourteen types have a minimum of 2 sub-types associated with them (the available sub-types frequently include 3D alternatives), often more, so all in all you're certain to find the chart that suits your data needs.

Available chart types

Below are details of some of the main chart types:

Column

Compares items or displays changes over time. Stacked and 3-D columns are good at emphasizing the relationship between individual items and the whole.

Bar

As above, but less emphasis on time. Values are displayed horizontally while categories are shown vertically.

Line

Best for displaying trends where time intervals are equal.

Area

Best for showing how parts relate to the whole, and for seeing the extent of changes when viewed over time. Area charts are especially visual and easy to take in.

XY (Scatter)

Best for plotting several data series, especially uneven ones. Bubble charts are a type of XY (Scatter). If you're not a science guru, these chart types are probably best avoided.

Pie

As Area, but only shows one data series. Use pie charts when you need to emphasize one specific data element.

In all graph types apart from XY (Scatter) and Bubble (where the first row or column holds data), the initial row and column in the Datasheet hold identifying text.

Doughnut

Doughnut charts resemble pie charts but show more than one data series. Each ring is one series.

Radar

Compares total values relating to several data series. Lines link all values in the same series.

Changing chart types

You can combine chart types in what PowerPoint calls "combination" charts. A common example is where bar and line chart types are combined so that the chart can display more than one information source. You combine types by applying more than one chart type to data series pre-selected before steps 1–6 on the right.

1 Double-click the chart in its host slide then hit Chart, Chart Type

2 Ensure the Standard Types tab is active

4 Click a sub-type

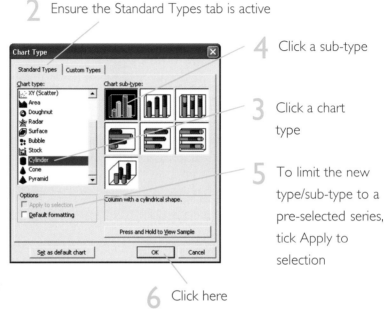

3 Click a chart type

5 To limit the new type/sub-type to a pre-selected series, tick Apply to selection

6 Click here

To specify a chart type as the default (so PowerPoint uses it automatically when you create a new chart), Select Set as default chart.

Customizing chart types

You can also apply customized chart types, professionally designed formats which incorporate colors, patterns and legends etc.

1 Activate the Custom Types tab in the above dialog

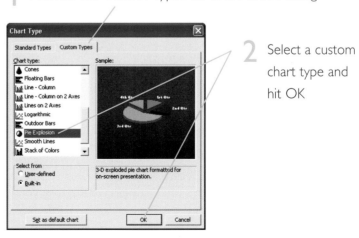

2 Select a custom chart type and hit OK

Creating your own chart types

You can create your own chart types (e.g. for distribution to coworkers).

1 Give the active chart the formatting you want then select it

2 Launch the Chart Type dialog (see the facing page) then hit the Custom Types tab

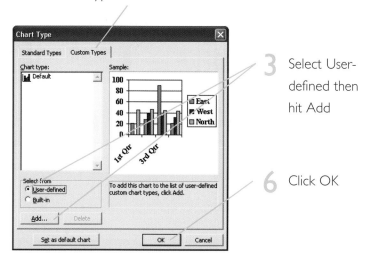

3 Select User-defined then hit Add

6 Click OK

4 Name the new chart type and (optionally) type in a description

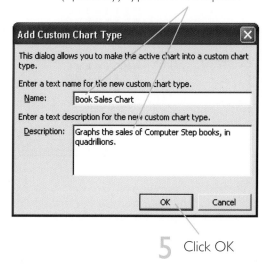

5 Click OK

Coloring chart components

After you've inserted a chart, you can select specific chart objects and apply a color or a texture/pattern fill. You can also change the line width/border style and apply a new typeface or type size.

Applying a color

In Normal view, go to the slide which hosts the chart you want to amend. Double-click the chart. Now do the following:

If you're recoloring text (for instance, the textual component of a legend), double-click it. In the dialog, select the Font tab. Click the Color box, then select a color in the list. Click OK.

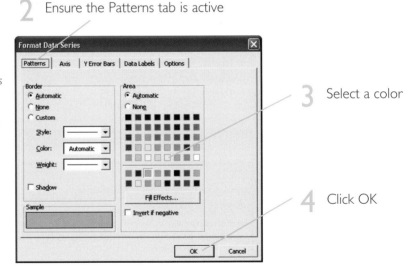

With the chart active, double-click the component you want to recolor (here, a data series)

2 Ensure the Patterns tab is active

Select another tab to achieve different effects (available options depend on the item selected). For example, choose Data Labels and specify what the chart's data labels should contain (series/category names, or values).

3 Select a color

4 Click OK

To insert a gradient, texture or pattern fill (or a fill involving a picture), hit the Fill Effects button and complete the Fill Effects dialog in the normal way.

5 To prevent your chart colors from automatically changing when you apply a new color scheme to your presentation, select your chart. Hit Format, Object. Select the Picture tab and hit Recolor. In the dialog, select None

Bordering chart components

Changing the line width/border style

1 In Normal view, go to the slide that hosts the chart you want to amend. Double-click the chart then the chart component you want to reformat

You can add text boxes to charts. Just drag with the Text Box tool on the Drawing toolbar (View, Toolbars, Drawing) in the usual way.

2 Ensure the Patterns tab is active

To format all text in a text box, right-click anywhere on its frame. (To format specific text, select it first inside the frame.) In the menu, click Font. Complete the Font dialog.

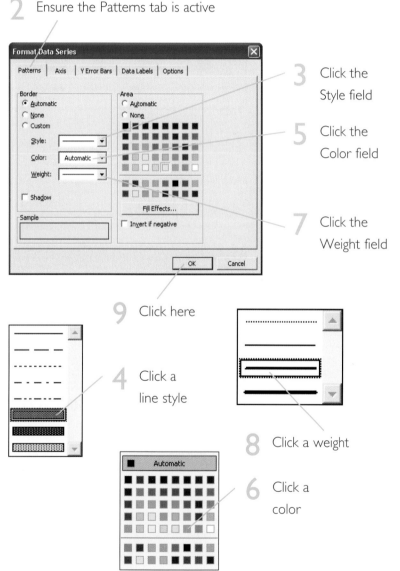

3 Click the Style field

5 Click the Color field

7 Click the Weight field

9 Click here

4 Click a line style

8 Click a weight

6 Click a color

Formatting text components

Applying a typeface/type size

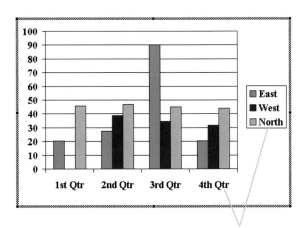

| With the chart active, double-click a text element (e.g. a legend or chart axis)

To align text in an axis, select the Alignment tab. Select a text orientation and direction and click OK.

2 Ensure the Font tab is active

3 Select a typeface

This dialog varies according to the text element you've selected.

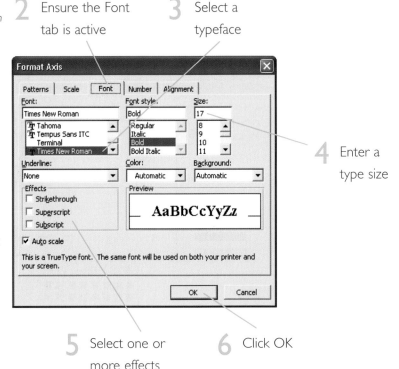

4 Enter a type size

Uncheck Auto scale to stop text and numerical data attached to a chart being automatically resized when you resize the chart.

5 Select one or more effects

6 Click OK

Using multimedia

Hey, why not spruce up your slides with pictures and clip art? In fact, this is more or less obligatory: slides with just text would be pretty boring. PowerPoint makes it easy to edit pictures, too – you can do lots of things (like cropping and changing brightness or contrast) that you'd normally have to do in your photo-editing software. Use the Clip Organizer to keep track of all your clip art. One way to do this is to give them all relevant keywords: this makes finding them again a breeze.

While you're at it, you can also add diagrams, organization charts, sound clips and movies to your presentations, for even more pizzazz.

Covers

Chapter Six

Multimedia – an overview

You can add impact to your slides by adding a variety of graphic and multimedia elements. In fact, slides wouldn't really be slides without these ingredients. Elements you can add include:

- clip art (via the Clip Art Task Pane or slide placeholders)

- output from other programs – for example, drawings, illustrations and scanned photographs

- diagrams

- organization charts

- sound clips

- video clips

Once you've inserted clip art and pictures, you can also animate them – see Chapter 8.

Clip Organizer

You can import sound clips, video clips and clip art via the Clip Organizer. This is a computerized scrapbook which helps you access (and organize) multimedia files. It's a centralized location from which you can interact with, and housekeep, your entire multimedia collection. You don't have to use the Clip Organizer to insert clips into slides but it does make it easier to locate the clip you want to use.

You can run this automatic cataloging process at any time – see step 7 on page 128.

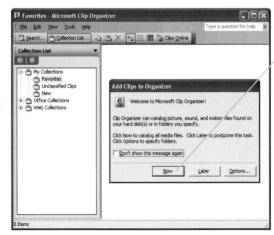

The Clip Organizer when it's just launched – click Now to catalog all the clips on your hard disk

Inserting clip art

Inserting clip art via the Clip Art Task Pane

1 In Normal or Notes Page views, go to the slide into which you want the clip art added then hit Insert, Picture, Clip Art

2 Enter one or more keywords

Clips have associated keywords. You can use these to locate clips.

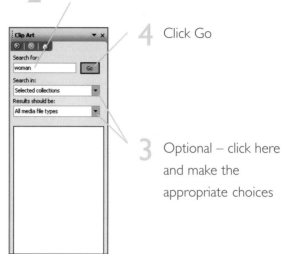

4 Click Go

3 Optional – click here and make the appropriate choices

5 Click an icon to insert the clip

6 In the slide, resize and reposition the picture in the normal way

For access to more clips, click Clip art on Office Online and follow the onscreen instructions.

Providing the relevant slide has an associated layout which incorporates a clip art placeholder, you can use this to make inserting an image even easier.

Adding clip art via placeholders

In some slide layouts, the Clip Art placeholder is one of a group.

I In Normal or Notes Page views, go to the slide into which you want the clip art added

2 Double-click here

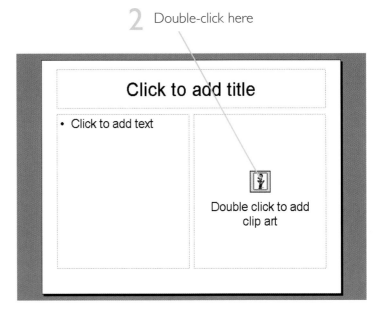

To find more clips, click Import. Use the Add Clips to Organizer dialog to locate and add more clips.

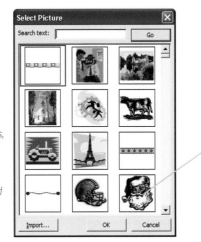

3 Double-click a clip

Working with the Clip Organizer

By default, the Clip Organizer comes with numerous predefined collections – for example, Business, Character Collections, Communication, Fantasy and People.

The Clip Organizer has lots of different sorts of clips. These include drawings (in Windows Metafile – .wmf – format), photographs, sounds and movies.

Launching the Clip Organizer

1 Launch the Clip Art Task Pane (Insert, Picture, Clip Art)

2 Hit Organize clips (this also works in any other Office 2003 program)

Inserting clips via the Organizer

Open the Clip Organizer (see page 125)

To remove a clip from the Organizer (but not your hard disk), right-click it. In the menu, click Delete from Clip Organizer. In the message which launches, click OK.

3 Drag a clip onto your slide

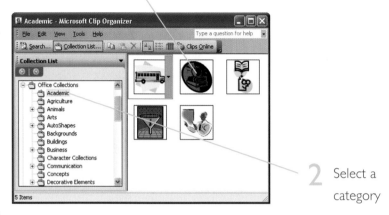

2 Select a category

To add an AutoShape or WordArt object (or any picture created in any other Office module) to the Organizer, select it. Press Ctrl+C. In the Organizer, go to the collection folder you want to add the object to and press Shift+Insert – a copy of the object is inserted as a clip.

4 Resize and/or reposition the picture in the usual way

More clips on Office Online

To access more clips on the Web, click the Clips Online button on the toolbar

2 Click a clip or category for more clips

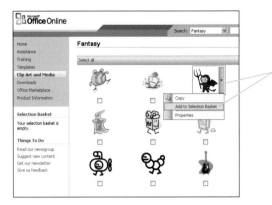

3 Click the clip you want and select Add to Selection Basket

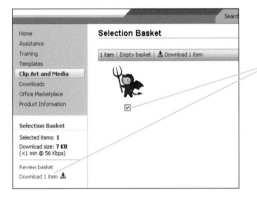

4 When you've chosen enough clips, make sure they're checked then hit Download...

5 Review your Selection Basket and hit Download Now – handle the download in the usual way

Creating new collections

You can only create a new collection from within "My Collections".

1 Launch the Clip Organizer

2 Click Collection List then select My Collections

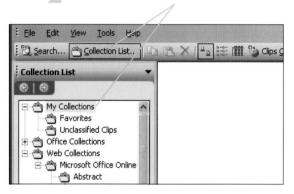

3 Hit File, New Collection

To preview a clip (you also get creation details and animations display in full), right-click it in the Organizer and select Preview/Property.

5 Name the collection

When Clip Organizer creates collections automatically, their names are based on the host folders. You can easily rename these.

4 Select a destination folder

6 Click here

To rename a collection, click a folder you've created under "My Collections" and hit F2. Overtype the old name and hit Enter.

7 To search for media files and organize them into collections, hit File, Add Clips to Organizer, Automatically. In the dialog, click OK. (When you start Organizer for the first time, it offers to carry out this procedure for you)

8 To manually add a clip to the Organizer, hit File, Add Clips to Organizer, On My Own. Use the dialog to locate and select the clip you want to add. Now click Add To. In the Import to Collection dialog, select a host collection

Adding keywords

When clips are added to the Clip Organizer, certain keywords are routinely added to them. These are based on the name or suffix, but it's a good idea to add your own keywords (so you can locate the clips more easily later).

Clips in the Clip Organizer can (and do) have keywords associated with them (this means, for instance, that if you want to find a specific picture you can run a keyword search – see page 130). You can add additional keywords to any clip you've added.

Associating keywords with a clip

1　Launch the Clip Organizer

2　Select a collection

To find related clips, select Find Similar Style in the contextual menu.

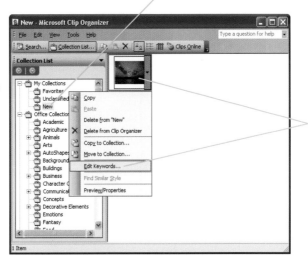

3　Right-click a clip; in the menu, select Edit Keywords

You can use a shortcut to email a clip to someone. Choose File, Send to Mail Recipient (as Attachment). Complete the New Message dialog and click Send.

4　Enter a new keyword and click Add – repeat as necessary

To change an existing keyword, select it in the dialog then hit Modify. Or hit Delete to remove it.

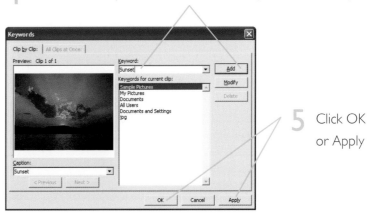

5　Click OK or Apply

Searching for keywords

To search for clips by one or more keywords:

1 Launch the Clip Organizer

2 Click Search   3 Enter keyword(s)

In the Search Task Pane, you can specify where Clip Organizer searches and what file type it looks for.

4 Click Go (if your Web connection is live, the search will find clips on Office Online)

Moving the mouse pointer over a clip produces a box listing the first few associated keywords.

Refining your search

Usually, finding a clip is straightforward but occasionally you'll need to pay especial attention to how you phrase your search.

1 You need to use a specific syntax in your searches. Base your syntax on the following examples:

- To find the keywords **red** and **bus**, type in: **red bus**
- To find the phrase **red bus**, type in: **"red bus"**
- To find red or bus, type in: **red, bus**

2 You can also search for filenames and use standard wildcards – for example, to find all BMP files, type in: ***.bmp**

Alternatively, to locate a clip called **plane1.tif** (but not **plane12.tif**), search for: **plane?.tif**

Pictures – an overview

PowerPoint 2003 lets you add color and grayscale pictures to slides. Pictures – also called graphics – include:

- drawings produced in other programs

- clip art

- photographs scanned in or imported from digital cameras (see page 133)

Pictures are stored in various third-party formats. These formats are organized into two basic types:

Bitmap images

Bitmaps consist of pixels (dots) arranged in such a way that they form a graphic image. Because of the very nature of bitmaps, the question of "resolution" – the sharpness of an image expressed in dpi (dots per inch) – is very important. Bitmaps look best if they're displayed at their correct resolution. PowerPoint 2003 can manipulate a wide variety of third-party bitmap graphics formats. These include: PCX, TIF, TGA and GIF.

Vector images

You can also insert vector graphics files into PowerPoint 2003 slides. Vector images consist of and are defined by algebraic equations. They're less complex than bitmaps and contain less detail. Vector files can also include bitmap information.

Irrespective of the format type, PowerPoint 2003 can incorporate pictures with the help of special "filters". These are special mini-programs whose job it is to translate third-party formats into a form which PowerPoint can use.

Compression

You can have PowerPoint compress images within slides (making them smaller).

See page 132 for details of bitmap and vector formats that PowerPoint 2003 recognizes.

1 In the Picture toolbar, click this button:

2 Complete the Compress Pictures dialog

Picture formats

Graphics formats PowerPoint 2003 will accept include the following (the column on the left shows the relevant file suffix):

BMP   Windows Bitmap. A popular bitmap format.

CGM   Computer Graphics Metafile. A vector format frequently used in the past, especially as a medium for clip-art transmission. Less often used nowadays.

EPS   Encapsulated PostScript. Perhaps the most widely used PostScript format. PostScript combines vector *and* bitmap data very successfully. Incorporates a low-resolution bitmap "header" for preview purposes.

GIF   Graphics Interchange Format. Developed for the online transmission of graphics data over the Internet. Just about any Windows program – and a lot more besides – will read GIF. There's one downside, though: it can't handle more than 256 colors. Compression is supported.

PCD   (Kodak) PhotoCD. Used primarily to store photographs on CD.

PCX   An old stand-by. Originated with PC Paintbrush, a paint program. Used for years to transfer graphics data between Windows applications.

TGA   Targa. A high-end format, and also a bridge with so-called low-end computers (e.g. Amiga and Atari). Often used in PC and Mac paint and ray-tracing programs because of its high-resolution color fidelity.

TIFF   Tagged Image File Format. Suffix: TIF. If anything, even more widely used than PCX, across a whole range of platforms and applications.

WMF   Windows Metafile. A frequently used vector format. Can be used for information exchange between just about all Windows programs.

Inserting pictures

To have a picture appear on every slide, insert it into the slide master. Hit View, Master, Slide Master then add a picture.

1 Position the insertion point at the location within the active slide where you want to insert the picture

2 Select Insert, Picture, From File

4 Click here. In the drop-down list, click the drive/folder that hosts the picture

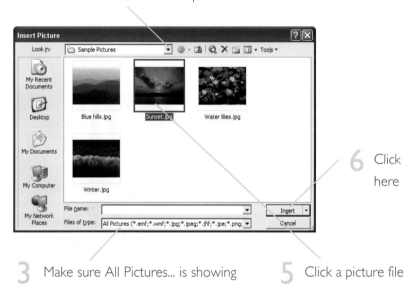

6 Click here

3 Make sure All Pictures... is showing

5 Click a picture file

Inserting pictures via scanners or cameras

1 Select Insert, Picture, From Scanner or Camera

Want to customize the acquisition? Click Custom Insert instead then complete your device's dialog.

You can only import from TWAIN-compliant devices.

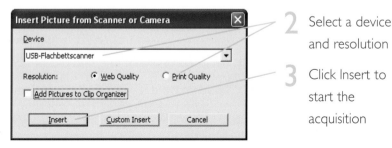

2 Select a device and resolution

3 Click Insert to start the acquisition

Editing clip art/pictures

Once you've inserted pictures into a PowerPoint 2003 slide, you can amend them in a variety of ways. First, you have to select the relevant picture. To do this, simply left-click once on an image. PowerPoint surrounds it with eight handles. The illustration below demonstrates these:

Handles   Rotate handle – drag to rotate

Only what PowerPoint calls "drawing objects" can be rotated – in other words, imported bitmaps such as photographs can't (do this instead in your photo-editing software).

If your image is not a bitmap and you still can't rotate it, try this. Select the image then make sure the Drawing toolbar (View, Toolbars, Drawing) is onscreen. Click on the Draw button and select Ungroup. Repeat but on this occasion select Group.

After this procedure, you can also use the drawing tools to change the colors.

1   To move a picture, just drag it to a new location

2   To rescale it, drag a corner handle to rescale proportionately, or a side handle to warp the image. Drag outwards to increase the size or inwards to reduce it

Complete any menu that launches after any of these steps (except for step 3 – you can use the dialog this produces to implement these and other changes).

Many of the effects applied to AutoShapes can also be applied to pictures. For example, you can shadow them and make them 3D...

Want to recolor bitmaps? You'll have to do this in your photo-editing software.

To crop from 2 sides at once, hold down Ctrl as you drag one center handle. To crop from all sides at once, Ctrl+drag a corner handle.

Using the Picture toolbar

When you import pictures or clip art, the Picture toolbar (View, Toolbars, Picture) should automatically launch. You can use this to make working with images even easier.

1 Adjust the color

2 More Contrast and Less Contrast

3 Launch the Format... dialog

4 More Brightness and Less Brightness

5 Crop the image (trim it or remove unwanted parts)

6 Recolor the image (but not bitmaps)

The image from the facing page:

- converted to "washout" (step 1) – this gives a watermark effect
- cropped (step 5)

By default, PowerPoint 2003 does not apply a border to inserted clip art/pictures. However, you can apply a wide selection of borders if you want. You can specify the border style and thickness, the border color and whether it's dashed.

Applying a border

1 Select the image you want to border then hit this icon in the Picture toolbar:

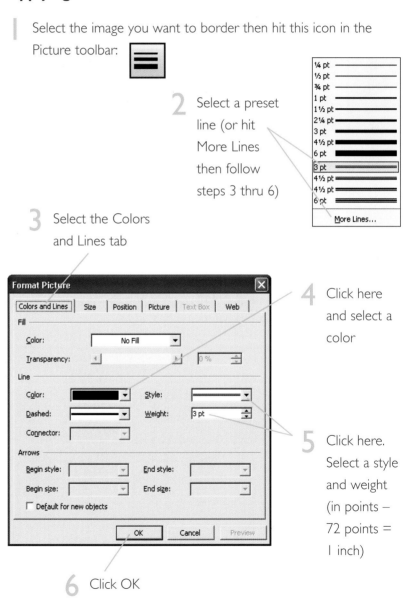

2 Select a preset line (or hit More Lines then follow steps 3 thru 6)

3 Select the Colors and Lines tab

4 Click here and select a color

To apply a dotted (as opposed to a straight) border, click in the Dashed field instead and select one in the list.

5 Click here. Select a style and weight (in points – 72 points = 1 inch)

6 Click OK

We saw on page 135 that you can increase brightness and contrast successively by clicking icons in the Picture toolbar. You can also do this by using a dialog box – this method is more accurate.

Amending brightness/contrast

1 Select the image you want to border then hit this icon in the Picture toolbar:

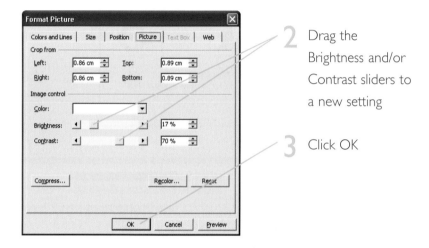

2 Drag the Brightness and/or Contrast sliders to a new setting

3 Click OK

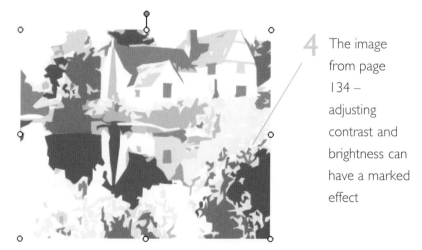

4 The image from page 134 – adjusting contrast and brightness can have a marked effect

Inserting diagrams

You can insert diagrams (e.g. pyramids) into slides.

1 In Normal or Notes Page view, pull down the Insert menu and click Diagram

Cycle   For continuous processes

Radial   Shows relationships between events and a central core

Pyramid   Best at showing "bottom-up" relationships

Venn   Best at showing overlapping areas

Target   Best at showing progressive steps

2 Select a diagram then hit OK

4 Make any further changes e.g. click Change to to convert to another diagram or Layout to make layout changes

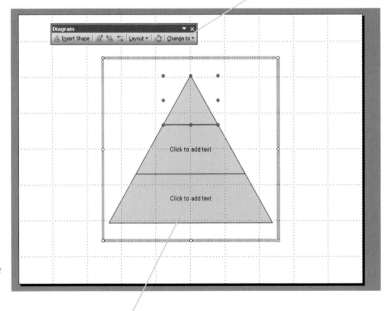

3 An inserted pyramid – edit it as required e.g. click a text placeholder and type in text, or resize it

Inserting organization charts

You can also insert organization charts into slides.

| Launch the Drawing toolbar (View, Toolbars, Drawing)

You can also create flowcharts via AutoShapes. Click AutoShapes on the Drawing toolbar then use the Flowchart, Lines and Connectors options.

2 Click this icon

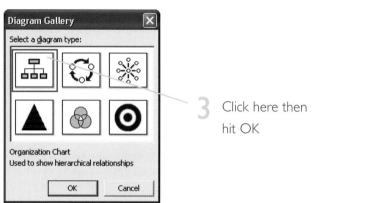

3 Click here then hit OK

4 PowerPoint inserts an organization chart

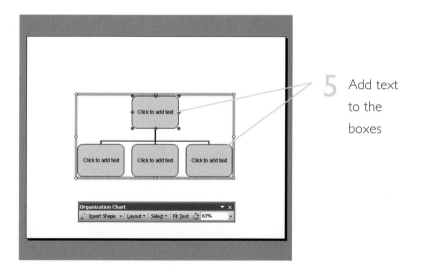

5 Add text to the boxes

Adding to organization charts

1 To extend the organization chart, refer to the Organization Chart toolbar and click this button's arrow: **Insert Shape** ▾

2 Select Coworker, Subordinate or Assistant

Changing the organization chart layout

1 To relay the organization chart, refer to the Organization Chart toolbar and click the arrow next to this button: **Layout ▾**

2 Select Standard, Both Hanging, Left Hanging or Right Hanging – this is Both Hanging

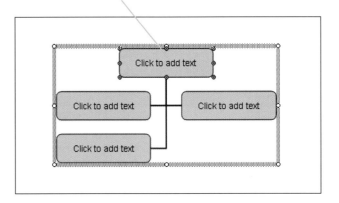

Formatting text in organization charts

1 To format organization chart text, select it then click the arrow next to this button in the Drawing toolbar: **A ▾**

2 In the fly-out, select a new color (from the associated color scheme) or hit More Colors then select one in the usual way

Downloading diagram templates

Office Online has some handy templates that you can download and use, free-of-charge, to create organization charts and planning diagrams. There are also links to PowerPoint training.

1 With your Internet connection live, hit F1

2 Type in "charts" and click the arrow

3 Click a template link

4 Click a training link

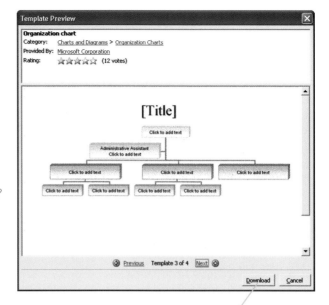

Want to see more templates? Hit the Previous or Next links.

5 This is a template – click here to download it

6 PowerPoint opens the new template – save it to disk

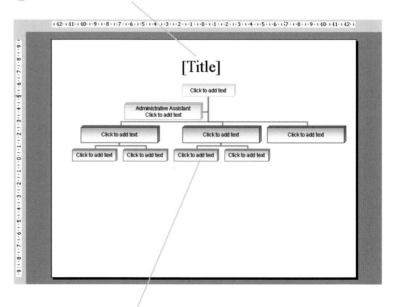

7 Click in the placeholders and type in your text

Inserting movies and sounds

1 In Normal or Notes Page views, go to the slide into which you want the movie or sound added

2 Ensure your Internet connection is live (for access to more movies or sounds)

3 Pull down the Insert menu and click Movies and Sounds. Select Movie from Clip Organizer or Sound from Clip Organizer

You can add movies and sounds from files, too. Just select Movie from File or Sound from File in the submenu then complete the dialog.

PowerPoint now supports lots of new file types with new features (for instance, you can play video full screen by right-clicking the movie, selecting Edit Movie Object and then clicking Zoom to full screen). These formats include Advanced Stream Redirector (.asx), Windows Media Redirector (.wvx) and Windows Media Audio Redirector (.wma).

If the required codec isn't installed on your system, PowerPoint and Media Player should download it automatically.

To manually play a video clip within a slide, simply double-click it.

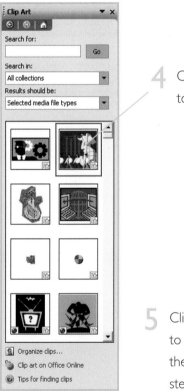

4 Click a movie to insert it

5 Click a sound to insert it then jump to step 6

6 Choose a delivery method

Playing tracks from audio CDs

You can play tracks from audio CDs during a presentation.

Inserting CD tracks

In Normal or Notes Page views, go to the slide into which you want the audio track added and choose Insert, Movies and Sounds, Play CD Audio Track

2 Select one or more tracks

3 Check this to loop playback

4 Adjust the volume

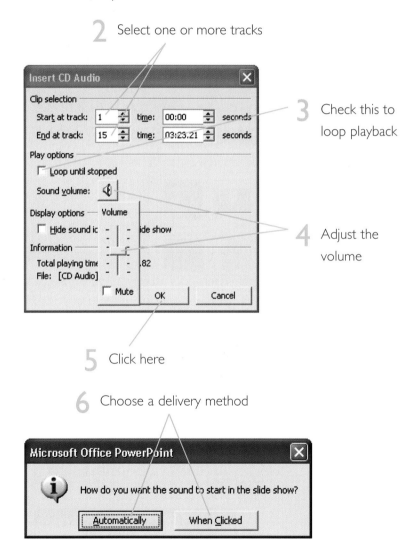

5 Click here

6 Choose a delivery method

Finalizing slide shows

When you stand up there and give your presentation, you likely will want to give your audience a handout that they can keep and use for future reference (or even make notes on). Hey, no problem in PowerPoint. You might need speaker notes, too, that you can use to make sure everything goes smoothly. And while you're into annotations, you can also insert comments into slides, either as memory aids or for coworkers to review.

When you create your handout, the options in PowerPoint mostly will be enough. However, if you need extra layout features, that's easy, too: you can export handouts to Word 2003. You can also print out straight slides for proofing.

Covers

Chapter Seven

Fine-tuning your slide show

When you've finished developing your presentation (using the techniques discussed in earlier chapters), you should consider adding some last minute enhancements before you get ready to run it. You can:

Summary slides list the main sections in your presentation for ease of access.

For how to create summary slides, see page 57.

- create summary slides
- insert internal comments
- add speaker notes
- create handouts

Comments

Internal comments aid the review/correction process by allowing presentations to be annotated by multiple users.

Speaker notes are a "script" which you can create in Notes Page view (or in Notes view within Normal view) to help you give the presentation. Many PowerPoint 2003 users find these scripts very useful, even indispensable.

Handouts

Handouts, on the other hand, are printed material which you supply to the slide show audience. Handouts consist of the following:

- an outline which the audience can follow as you speak
- copies of the individual slides (printed one or more to the page)

Additional preparations

These include:

- specifying page setup parameters
- specifying printer setup parameters
- printing out a proof copy of the presentation
- exporting slides or outlines to Word 2003

Comments – an overview

If your presentation needs to be reviewed, you can insert the necessary comments into the relevant slides. When you've done this, other users can review your annotations. Alternatively, you can simply insert comments for your own information. For example, if you're not sure about the design of a particular slide but want to move on to the next, you could insert a comment (for your own attention) as a reminder that you need to go back to the original slide and review it later . . .

PowerPoint 2003 comments are self-formatting, self-wrapping text boxes with associated markers:

Comment marker

| C2 | **Copestake** | **01/18/2004** |

Hi Shelley,

What do you think of this presentation? Is it cool, or what?|

If anyone else edits your comment, their initials are inserted and PowerPoint then regards them as the author of the comment.

When you create a comment, PowerPoint 2003 automatically inserts your name – in bold – at the start. When you type in the comment text, the box wraps around the text.

Fine-tuning comments

When you've inserted comments, you can:

* resize them

* edit them

* view/hide them

* delete them if they've been actioned and are no longer required

Inserting a comment

1 In Normal view, go to the slide into which you want to insert the comment

2 Hit Insert, Comment (all prior comments become visible)

3 PowerPoint 2003 inserts a new comment, complete with your name as the author

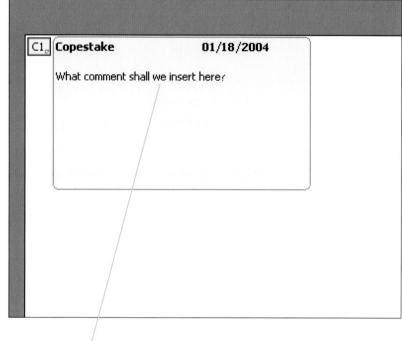

To print comments, launch the Print dialog (Ctrl+P). Check "Print comments and ink markup".

| C1 | **Copestake** | **01/18/2004** |

What comment shall we insert here?

4 Type in your comment, then click outside the comment box

5 To reposition a comment, drag its marker to another location

6 To resize a (completed) comment box, use standard Windows resizing techniques

7 To print out pages containing comments, select "Include comment pages" in the Print dialog

Working with comments

Viewing/hiding comment markers

To show or hide comments globally, you can also hit View, Markup.

To make comment markers visible or invisible (globally), click here in the Reviewing toolbar (View, Toolbars, Reviewing)

Viewing specific comments

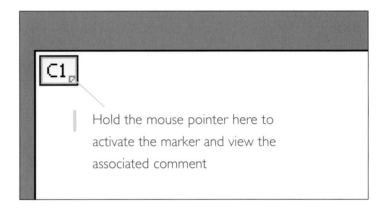

Hold the mouse pointer here to activate the marker and view the associated comment

Deleting comments

Click a comment marker and hit Delete – deletion is immediate

Editing comments

To delete all comments, click the arrow next to this button on the Reviewing toolbar (see below) then select Delete All Markup on the Current Slide or Delete All Markup in this Presentation:

To edit a comment, double-click its marker. Click in the comment then make the necessary changes. When you've finished, click back in the slide

Navigating comments

To view previous or subsequent comments, click these icons respectively in the Reviewing toolbar:

Working with speaker notes

Every PowerPoint 2003 slide has a corresponding Notes page which displays a reduced-size version of the slide and a notes section complete with a notes placeholder.

You can use the placeholder to enter notes which you'll refer to (either onscreen or from a printed copy) as you give your presentation.

You can create notes in the following ways:

If you have trouble working with note placeholders, try increasing the Zoom size. Hit View, Zoom then click a higher zoom percentage.

- from within Notes Page view

- from within Normal view

Adding speaker notes within Notes Page view

If you're not already using Notes Page view, hit View, Notes Page then go to the slide into which you want to enter notes

To print notes, carry out step 7 on page 160 (but select Notes Pages in the drop-down list).

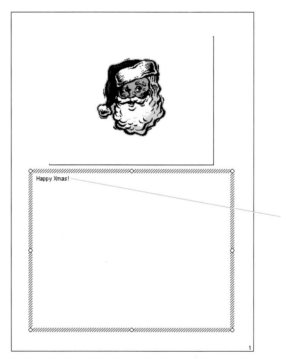

Happy Xmas!

3 Feel free to add extra pictures to your notes page (they won't display in Normal view)

2 Type in your notes then click outside the placeholder – the text size self-adjusts

Adding speaker notes within Normal view

1 If you're not already using Normal view, hit View, Normal

2 Go to the slide into which you want to enter notes

When you export presentations as Web pages, notes display automatically (they act like a speaker in a standard presentation).

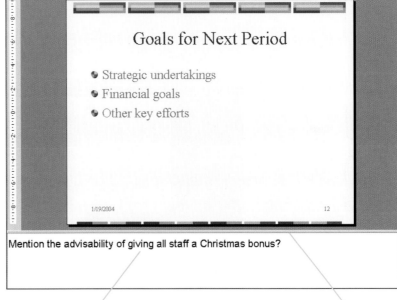

You can apply color schemes to notes and handouts.

4 Type in the
note text

3 Enlarge the note area
by dragging this bar

5 To add text or pictures to all notes pages, add them to the Notes master. Hit View, Master, Notes Master. Click in the note placeholder then add text and/or a picture in the normal way

6 To view note formatting accurately (as above), click this button in the Standard toolbar:

Handouts

Create handouts for two purposes: for the use of your audience, or for your own benefit while you give the presentation.

Creating a handout

1. Hit View, Master, Handout Master

2. PowerPoint 2003 now launches the Handout master with specific items (for instance, page numbers and footer text) already included

3. Replace <header> with header text and date/time with a specific date/time

By default, handouts have a white background. To change this, hit Format, Handout Background. Select a background color or fill in the usual way.

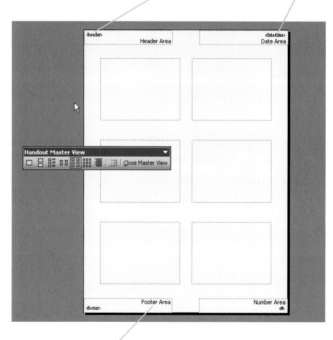

4. Add the relevant footer text

5. To specify the number of slides per page in the Handout master, click the icon which corresponds to the number:

To print handouts, launch the Print dialog (Ctrl+P). Click in the Print what box and select Handouts.

Some handouts include lines for note taking

Exporting handouts to Word 2003

If the procedures listed on the facing page aren't adequate (for instance, if the presentation you're developing also involves a manual), you can create your handout in Word. When you do this, PowerPoint 2003 transfers all notes/slides automatically while letting you choose the handout format. You can then use the greater formatting capabilities innate in Word 2003 to produce the handout you need.

Exporting to Word 2003

1 Hit File, Send To, Microsoft Office Word

 You can also send an outline to Word 2003. First ensure it shows the correct levels (by promoting/demoting etc. as necessary – see pages 54 thru 57). Now select Outline only in step 2.

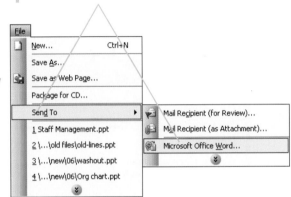

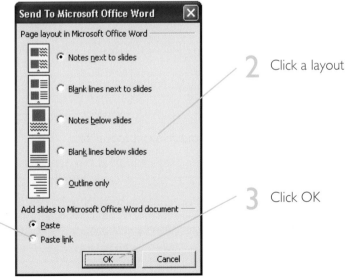

2 Click a layout

3 Click OK

If you want your slide show updated to take account of any changes you make in Word 2003 (see page 154), click Paste link:

4 PowerPoint 2003 now starts Word (if it isn't already running) and inserts your presentation (with the requested layout) into a new document

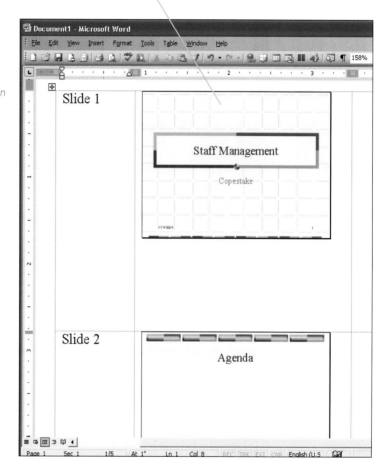

5 Edit the presentation in the normal way

6 If you clicked Paste link on page 153, any editing changes you make in Word are automatically reflected in your original presentation

Page setup issues

Before you print a slide show, it's a good idea to specify whether you want to print slides in Landscape (the default) or Portrait format. You should also set the page dimensions.

There are two aspects to every page size: a vertical measurement and a horizontal measurement. These can be varied according to orientation. There are two possible orientations:

If you change a slide show's orientation, you may have to adjust items on the slides (e.g. text placeholders) to accommodate the new orientation.

Portrait   Landscape

Specifying page setup options

Use this procedure to create transparencies.

1 Hit File, Page Setup

2 Click here; select a slide size in the list (hit Custom to define your own size)

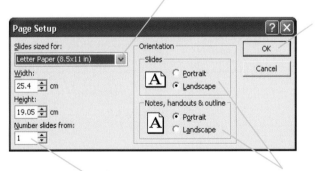

5 Click here

3 Type in a start slide number

4 Specify an orientation (all slides within a presentation must have the same one)

Printer setup

Before you can begin printing out your slide shows, you need to ensure that:

- the correct printer is selected (if you have more than one installed)

- the printer's settings are correct

PowerPoint 2003 calls these collectively the "printer setup".

Irrespective of the printer selected, the settings vary in accordance with the job in hand. For example, most printer drivers (the software which "drives" the printer) allow you to specify whether or not you want pictures printed. Additionally, they often allow you to specify the resolution or print quality of the output...

Selecting the printer and/or settings

1 At any time before you're ready to print a presentation, hit Ctrl+P or hit File, Print

2 Click here; select the printer you want from the list

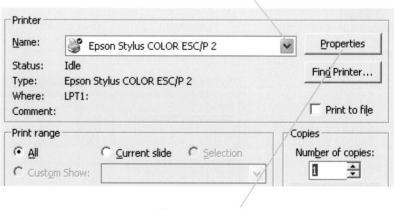

3 Click Properties to adjust printer settings

4 Select a tab then specify the necessary settings (your dialog box will probably look different)

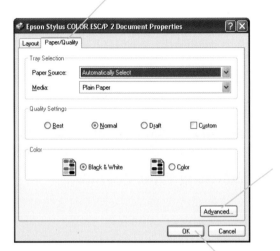

5 Click here to set advanced features

Different printers have different options – if in doubt, consult your printer's manual.

8 Click here

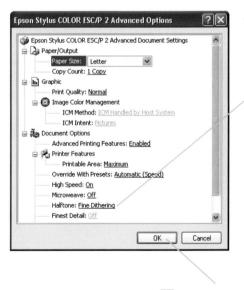

6 The advanced feature set may include toggling options like Microweave or setting halftoning options

7 Click OK

Launching Print Preview

Print Preview displays slides in grayscale if you're outputting to a grayscale printer.

PowerPoint 2003 provides a special view mode called Print Preview. This displays the active slide as it will look when printed. Use Print Preview as a final check just before you begin printing.

You can perform the following actions from within Print Preview:

- moving from slide to slide

- zooming in or out with the mouse pointer

- zooming to a preset view percentage

- specifying which component prints (you can also do this from the Print dialog – see page 160)

Launching Print Preview

1   Hit Ctrl+F2 (repeat to close Print Preview)

2   Use the toolbar to manipulate Print Preview – see the facing page

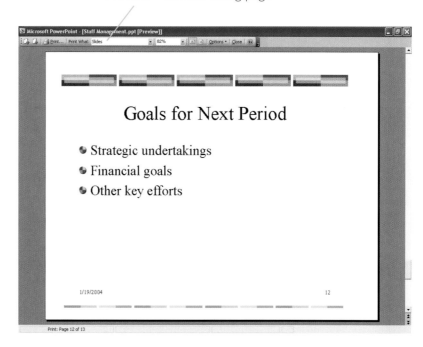

Working with Print Preview

Nearly all of the operations you can perform in Print Preview mode can be accessed via the toolbar.

Using the Print Preview toolbar

Do any of the following, as appropriate:

To print a frame around slides, click the Options button. In the menu, select Frame Slides.

1 Click here to jump to the next slide

3 Click here – in the list, select a Zoom size

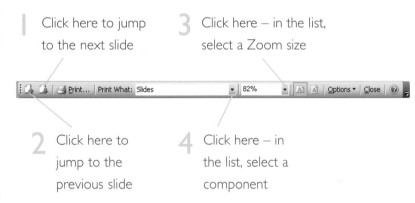

2 Click here to jump to the previous slide

4 Click here – in the list, select a component

Click Options in the toolbar then select Color/ Grayscale. In the menu, choose from the following options:

Pure Black and White	*Self-explanatory*
Grayscale	*Not all grayscales display (so you can read all the slide text)*
Color...	*PowerPoint displays true grayscales*

These commands do not change anything in the original presentation: they just affect printing.

Using the Zoom cursor

You can also zoom in or out (in a relatively limited way) by using the Zoom cursor.

1 Place the cursor at the appropriate location and left-click once to zoom in or out

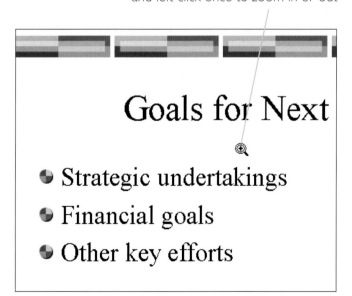

Printing your slide show

1 Hit Ctrl+P

2 Click here; select a printer

3 Click here to print the current slide only

Collation prints one full copy at a time. For instance, if you're printing three copies of a 10-slide presentation, PowerPoint prints slides 1 thru 10 of the first copy, followed by slides 1 thru 10 of the second and so on.

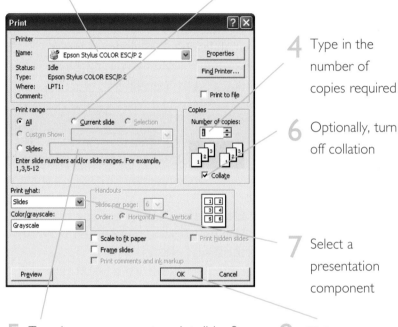

4 Type in the number of copies required

6 Optionally, turn off collation

Ensure "Grayscale" and "Pure Black and White" are deselected in Color/grayscale if you have a color printer and want to print out in color.

7 Select a presentation component

Presentations are intended to be printed in color; however, handouts and notes are generally printed in grayscale or mono.

5 Type in a range – e.g. to print slides 2, 5 and 9 type in "2,5,9". To print slides 2 thru 7, type in "2-7" (no quotes)

8 Click here

Fast-track printing

To print out immediately with the default formatting, hit this button in the Standard toolbar:

Disabling background printing

Background printing takes up additional system resources. To disable this, hit Tools, Options. Select the Print tab and uncheck Background printing

Preparing slide shows

Hey, you're almost ready to give your presentation now! You just need to apply transitions to your slides – in other words, you tell PowerPoint exactly how each slide should appear and disappear. You can also pep up transitions by applying animations to objects on your slides. It's a good idea to insert hyperlinks, too: these make it a lot easier to navigate to other slides, files or Web/intranet addresses. After this, why not create custom shows (great if you want to adapt a base presentation for use in different circumstances)?

Finally, you'll rehearse your presentation, to make sure everything works as it should.

Covers

Chapter Eight

Preparation – an overview

See Chapter 9 for how to perform (run) slide shows.

There's a whole tranche of techniques you can use to ensure that your presentation has the maximum impact. These are all ways of preparing your slide show for its eventual performance.

You can:

- specify transitions (interactions between individual slides)

- apply animations (used to control how each slide element is introduced to the audience)

- insert hyperlinks (buttons/objects which – when clicked – jump to additional slides or other targets)

- customize slide timings (the intervals between slides)

- customize the presentations setup

Presentation setup

You can specify:

- which slides do or do not display (via custom slide shows). Use this to prepare presentations which are tailored for specific audiences (some slides may not be suitable for a given recipient) and add hyperlinks where appropriate

- the type of slide show delivery. You can decide whether the presentation runs normally (i.e. you as the presenter orchestrate it), in a special window or at a conference kiosk

- whether the presentation runs in "loop" mode

- if slides are advanced manually or using the preset timings

- an alternative screen resolution

- (if you have dual-monitor support) which monitor a presentation runs on

Transitions

Transitions add visual interest to presentations by customizing the crossover between individual slides. PowerPoint 2003 provides numerous separate transition effects. These include:

Random Transition	PowerPoint 2003 selects and applies the transition
Blinds Horizontal or Vertical	The next slide displays like a blind
Checkerboard Across or Down	The next slide displays with a checkered pattern
Box In or Out	The next slide displays as an increasing or decreasing box

When you apply a transition to a specific slide, the effect takes place between the previous and selected slides.

You can specify transition effects:

*   on all slides within a presentation

*   on individual slides

Applying transitions to the whole of a slide show

In any view, hit Slide Show, Slide Transition

In Normal view, to restrict a transition to the active slide, select it on the right.

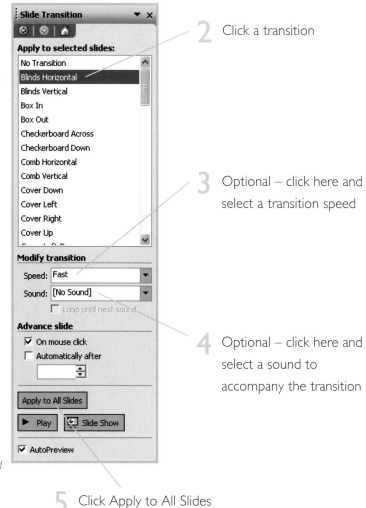

2 Click a transition

3 Optional – click here and select a transition speed

4 Optional – click here and select a sound to accompany the transition

When AutoPreview is checked, clicking a transition in the "Apply to selected slides" section previews the effect in the slide itself.

5 Click Apply to All Slides

Applying transitions to specific slides

In Slide Sorter view (View, Slide Sorter), Ctrl+click to select multiple slides then apply transitions as above

Animations

You can use animations to:

- introduce objects onto a slide one at a time (by default, they all appear onscreen at once)

- apply special effects to objects

You can have too much of a good thing. Bear the following guidelines in mind:

- don't use too many custom animations
- keep animated objects small rather than large
- use solid-color fills (rather than gradients) in animated objects

Having objects appear in a staggered way maximizes slide impact; the eye is drawn to areas of specific interest in a way which makes them more prominent.

Imposing special effects on objects is particularly useful when you need individual items in a bulleted list to appear one at a time or to have pictures, clip art or charts become prominent slowly.

You can apply preset animation schemes or create your own.

Applying an animation scheme

Hit Slide Show, Animation Schemes

2 Click an animation scheme to apply it to the active slide or multiple slides (if you pre-selected them in Slide Sorter view)

3 Additionally, to apply the animation to every slide click Apply to All Slides

Customizing animations

1 In Normal view, right-click the object you want to animate and select Custom Animation in the menu

2 Click Add Effect (you can also use this technique to animate diagrams and organization charts)

4 Configure these fields

In step 3, optionally select Motion Paths and select a path.

3 In the menus, select an effect type then a specific animation

The tags correlate with the animations listed on the right.

6 Animations display as non-printing tags against the relevant object

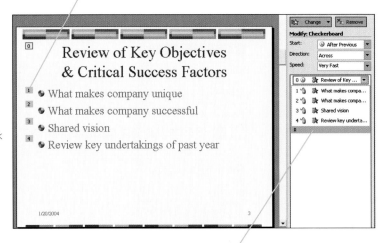

To remove an animation, right-click it in the Task Pane and select Remove.

5 Click here to view animations in order

Previewing and editing animations

1 In Normal view, hit Slide Show, Custom Animation

Previewing also plays any associated sound tracks.

2 In the Custom Animation Task Pane, hit this button:

3 PowerPoint runs thru all animations in the slide – watch the timeline

To recolor animation text after an animation, right-click the item in the Task Pane and select Effect Options. In the dialog, hit the Effect tab. Click in "After animation" and apply a color in the usual way.

You can also use the dialog to apply a sound to an animation: click in the Sound field and choose one.

4 To customize an animation even further, right-click it. In the menu, select Effect Options. Select the Effect tab and complete the dialog. For instance, to set an animation's timings, select the Timing tab and make any changes

5 To change the sequence of animations, select one in the Task Pane and drag it to a new location in the list

6 To amend an animation's type, select it in the Task Pane. Click Change and apply a new effect

7 To remove an animation, select its entry in the Task Pane then hit Remove in the menu

Inserting hyperlinks

You can insert hyperlinks into slides. Hyperlinks are "action buttons" which you can click (while a presentation is being run) to jump to a prearranged destination immediately. This can be:

Text, charts, images and WordArt objects can also be hyperlinks, but action buttons are convenient, ready-made solutions (they're especially suitable for continually running slide shows).

To make any other object a hyperlink, select it. Choose Slide Show, Action Settings. Now follow steps 4 thru 7.

- preset slide targets (e.g. the first, last, next or previous slide)

- a specific slide (where you select a slide from a dialog)

- a URL (Uniform Resource Locator – unique addresses for websites or intranet locations)

- another PowerPoint presentation or file

Add action buttons to masters to have them appear on multiple slides or insert them into the active slide.

Inserting an action button

Action buttons are actually AutoShapes (refer to pages 100 thru 103).

1 In Normal or Notes Page view, hit Slide Show, Action Buttons then select a button

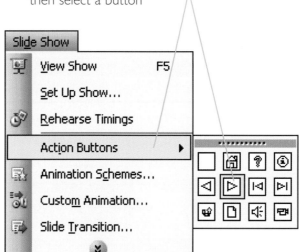

You can also have action buttons (or other objects) launch external programs in the course of a presentation.

Select the button/object. Pull down the Slide Show menu and click Action Settings. Select Run program and use the Browse button to locate and double-click the relevant program file.

2 Drag out the button (Shift+drag to retain its width/height ratio)

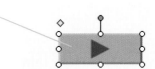

3 In the dialog, select the Mouse Click or Mouse Over tab (Mouse Click means you have to click the button to use the hyperlink; Mouse Over means you can just pass the pointer over it)

Typing an email or Web address on a slide creates a hyperlink automatically.

4 Click Hyperlink to:

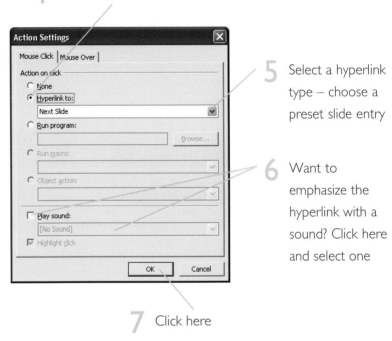

5 Select a hyperlink type – choose a preset slide entry

6 Want to emphasize the hyperlink with a sound? Click here and select one

7 Click here

Editing hyperlinks

Hyperlinks only become active when you run your slide show.

Text hyperlinks are underlined.

1 Make a point of frequently checking and repairing hyperlinks, especially just before you run your presentation

2 Right-click the hyperlink and select Edit Hyperlink

3 Complete the Action Settings dialog. (To delete the hyperlink, select Remove Hyperlink)

Specifying slide timing

You can specify how long each slide is onscreen, and by implication the duration of the entire presentation. There are two ways to do this:

- from within Slide Sorter view (singly or for every slide)

- by "rehearsing" the presentation

Applying timings in Slide Sorter view

1   Select one or more slides

2   Pull down the Slide Show menu and click Slide Transition

3   Type in a time (in seconds) and press Enter

4   Click Apply to All Slides to have the timing applied to every slide

...cont'd

Rehearsing slides uses a special PowerPoint 2003 feature called the Slide Meter.

Applying timings with the Slide Meter

1 In any view, hit Slide Show, Rehearse Timings

When you've set timings, you can turn them off (this doesn't delete them). Follow step 1 on page 174. In the dialog, select Manually in the Advance slides section. (To reinstate timings, select Using timings, if present.)

2 PowerPoint launches its rehearsal window. This is very similar to the screen you get when you run a presentation – the difference is that the Slide Meter displays as well as the first slide

3 This timer counts the interval until the next slide; when the timing is right, follow step 4

You can also enter times manually.

4 Click here – if a slide has custom animations, this command steps through each before moving on to the next slide

5 PowerPoint moves to the next slide. Repeat steps 3 and 4 until all the slides have had intervals allocated

6 Click Yes

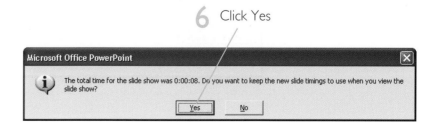

Custom slide shows

PowerPoint 2003 lets you create custom slide shows. Custom shows let you adopt a mix-and-match approach by selecting specific slides from the active presentation. This way, you can tailor a presentation for specific audiences or occasions.

Creating a custom show

1 Select one or more slides then hit Slide Show, Custom Shows

2 Click New

6 Click Close

3 Name the show

4 Double-click slides to add them

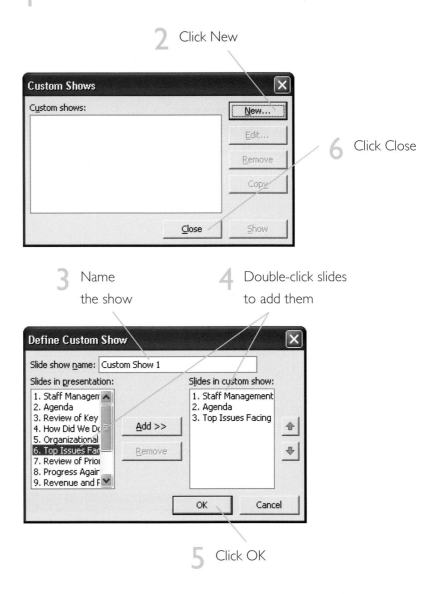

5 Click OK

Once you've set up a custom slide show, you can add or remove slides and move them up or down.

Editing a custom show

Use hyperlinks to link to shows that are subsets of the main custom show (select Custom Show in step 5 on page 169). For example, create a table of contents with links to separate presentation sections.

1 Pull down the Slide Show menu and click Custom Shows

2 Click a custom show

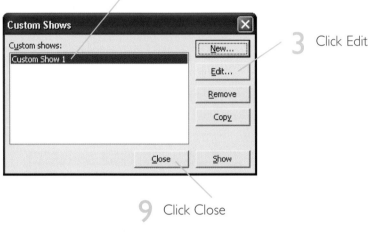

3 Click Edit

9 Click Close

4 Click a slide

To add a new slide to the custom show, double-click it in the field on the left of the dialog box.

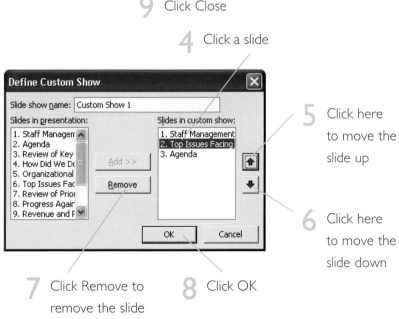

5 Click here to move the slide up

6 Click here to move the slide down

7 Click Remove to remove the slide

8 Click OK

Final preparations

You're now at the last stage in slide show preparation. This involves telling PowerPoint 2003:

- the type of presentation you want to run

- whether you want it to run perpetually

- whether you want each slide to appear automatically

Setting up a presentation

If your PC is set up for dual-monitor support (this means having the correct hardware and Windows 98 or later), you can choose the monitor you'll use to display the slide show. Select it in the Multiple monitors section of the Set Up Show dialog.

1 Hit Slide Show, Set Up Show

2 Click a slide show type – for a continually running slide show, check "Browsed at a kiosk (full screen)" and "Loop continuously until Esc" below

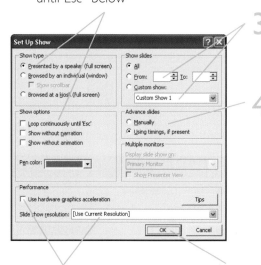

3 Specify which slides run or select a custom slide show

4 Select Manually to control slide transition or "Using timings, if present" for the transition to follow the timings you set on pages 170–171

5 Choose a lower resolution (and/or check "Use hardware graphics acceleration") to improve slide show performance

6 Click OK

Presenting slide shows

Now it's party time – you're ready to present your slide show to a live audience. There are lots of techniques for making this easier, more productive and fun. You can use keyboard commands or the mouse to navigate through your presentation. You can also annotate your slides temporarily with the Ballpoint, Felt Tip or Highlighter pens – this technique makes it a lot easier to get your point across.

Covers

Chapter Nine

Running your presentation

Another scenario involves a self-running presentation in a kiosk – this needs little or no user involvement.

By now, your presentation is ready to run. PowerPoint lets you:

- present it to a live audience (this is the most common scenario)

- create a special file enabling slide shows to be run on PCs that don't have PowerPoint 2003 installed – see pages 73 thru 74

- publish your slide show on the World Wide Web, using Microsoft's enhanced HTML format (see page 66 for more information). This means that anyone with Internet Explorer 4 or above can run it in a way which – since the original formatting is preserved with high fidelity – is more or less identical to the first option. So users can run your presentation without having to have PowerPoint 2003

Running standard slide shows live

Select Slide Show, View Show (if you set up your presentation appropriately – see Chapter 8 – this will also start a self-running or dual-monitor presentation)

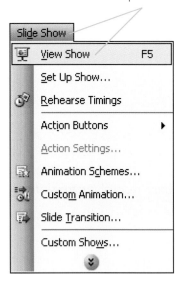

2 Alternatively, hit F5

3 PowerPoint 2003 launches the first slide in a special window:

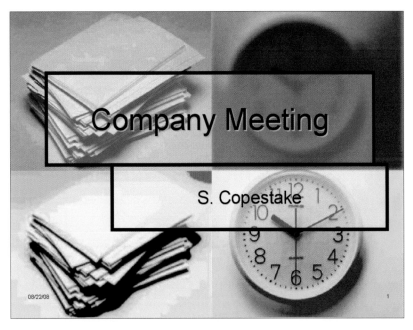

Any movies or sounds you've inserted into slides should play automatically when you run the presentation.

4 If you allocated slide timings (using one of the techniques on pages 170 thru 171) and selected "Using timings, if present" (in step 4 on page 174), PowerPoint 2003 displays the next slide automatically

5 If, on the other hand, you selected Manually in step 4 on page 174, left-click once to view the next slide – repeat as necessary

6 If you're using manual progression, you can also use the keystrokes listed on page 179

Running custom slide shows live

1 Hit Slide Show, Custom Shows

2 Select a custom show

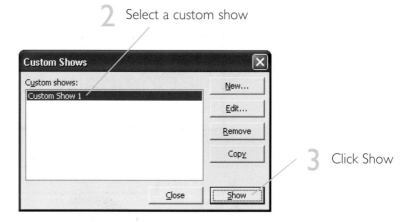

3 Click Show

4 The presentation runs and the first slide displays:

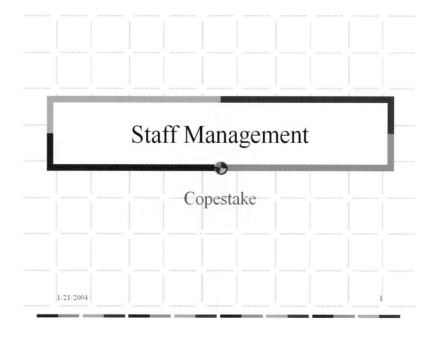

Navigating through slide shows

Navigating – the keystroke approach

When you run a presentation, you're actually using a special view called Slide Show. There are special commands you can use to move around in Slide Show view. Press any of the keystrokes listed in the left column to produce the desired result (on the right):

Enter; Page Down; or the Spacebar	jumps to the next slide
Page Up or Backspace	jumps to the previous slide
B or full stop	toggles a black screen
W or comma	toggles a white screen
"Slide number" plus Enter	goes to the specified slide
S	stops/restarts an automatic slide show (i.e. one where the presenter is not initiating slide progression manually)
Home	jumps to the first slide
End	jumps to the last slide
Esc	ends a slide show

Navigating – the mouse approach

You can also use mouse actions:

Single left-click	jumps to the next slide
Single right-click	produces a helpful menu – for example, hit Go to Slide then select a slide in the extra menu

PowerPoint 2003 has a dedicated toolbar you can use to help you present your slide show. The Slide Show toolbar is unobtrusive, even subtle, so it won't be obvious to your audience yet it provides access to the features you'll use most often.

Using the Slide Show toolbar

When you're running the presentation, rest the mouse pointer on the slide to display the toolbar

If the toolbar is elusive, make sure it's enabled. Choose Tools, Options. Select the View tab and check Show popup toolbar.

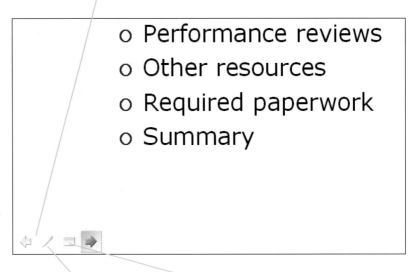

o **Performance reviews**

o **Other resources**

o **Required paperwork**

o **Summary**

Use the toolbar arrows to step back and forward thru the slides (especially when annotating them).

2 Click here to produce this menu:

3 Click here to produce this menu:

When you run a slide show, PowerPoint displays an arrow as a pointer – it's hidden after 3 seconds of inactivity and reappears when you move the mouse. To display the arrow all the time, right-click and select Arrow Options followed by Visible.

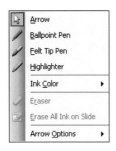

| Arrow |
| Ballpoint Pen |
| Felt Tip Pen |
| Highlighter |
| Ink Color ▶ |
| Eraser |
| Erase All Ink on Slide |
| Arrow Options ▶ |

| Next |
| Previous |
| Last Viewed |
| Go to Slide ▶ |
| Custom Show ▶ |
| Screen ▶ |
| Help |
| Pause |
| End Show |

Emphasizing slide shows

PowerPoint 2003 lets you emphasize slides during a live presentation. You do this by using various pens. When you've finished annotating slides, you can opt to discard your doodles (the usual choice) or you can keep them.

Setting the ink color

The first stage is to tell PowerPoint what color ink to use. The color you set is pen-specific.

1 In Slide Show view, right-click anywhere on screen

2 Select the pen or highlighter you want to use (see overleaf)

Marks you make with the pens or highlighter are only temporary: they disappear when you move to another slide.

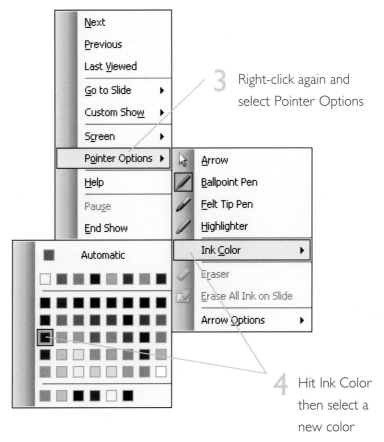

3 Right-click again and select Pointer Options

4 Hit Ink Color then select a new color

Using the pens

In Slide Show view, right-click anywhere on screen

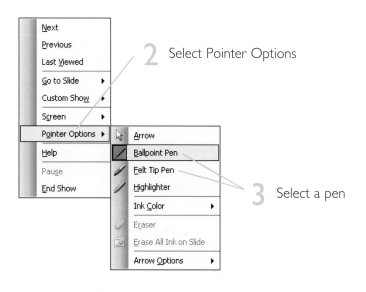

2 Select Pointer Options

3 Select a pen

This is the Felt Tip Pen in action.

To-Do List

- Our goal is to make pots of money
- Get rid of deadwood by downsizing
- Make everyone's cubicle smaller!!!

4 Draw with the selected pen – hit Esc when you're thru

Using the highlighter

1 In Slide Show view, right-click anywhere on screen

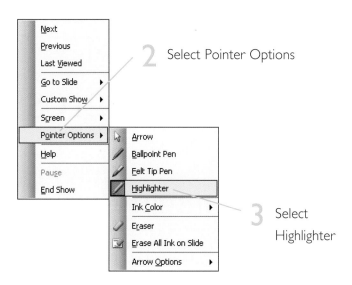

2 Select Pointer Options

3 Select Highlighter

4 Draw with the highlighter – hit Esc when you're thru

After you've pressed Esc, a message appears. Hit Keep to retain your annotations or Discard to lose them.

If you've saved your annotations, hit View, Markup in Normal or Slide Sorter view to display or hide them.

To-Do List

- Our goal is to make pots of money
- Get rid of deadwood by downsizing
- Make everyone's cubicle smaller

Erasing annotations

If you make a mistake while you're annotating a slide, you can correct it on-the-fly.

1 After the error, right-click and select Pointer Options, Eraser

Progress Agains

Summary of key <u>financial</u>

- Revenue
- Profit
- Key spending areas
- Headcount

2 Click the annotation to remove it

3 Alternatively, to get rid of all annotations right-click and select Pointer Options, Erase All Ink on Slide. Or just press E

Running presentations in Explorer

One corollary of Microsoft's elevation of the HTML format to a status which rivals that of its own formats (see page 66) is that:

- presentations display authentically in Internet Explorer (especially if you're using version 4 or above)

- you can even run presentations from within Internet Explorer

Running slide shows in Internet Explorer

1 Use the relevant techniques discussed on page 69 to convert an existing presentation to HTML format

2 Open the Web presentation in Internet Explorer:

3 Toggle the outline on or off

4 Click Slide Show to run your show in Full-Screen mode

5 Internet Explorer now launches the first slide of your presentation so that it occupies the whole screen:

Staff Management

Copestake

1/21/2004   1

To halt the slide show before the end, press Esc.

6 If you allocated slide timings (using one of the techniques on pages 170 thru 171) and selected "Using timings, if present" (in step 4 on page 174) , PowerPoint 2003 progresses to the next slide when the set interval has elapsed

7 If, on the other hand, you selected Manually in step 4 on page 174, left-click once to view the next slide – repeat as necessary

8 When the last slide has been displayed, a special screen displays with the following text:

End of slide show, click to exit.

9 Click anywhere to return to Internet Explorer's main screen

Index

N

O

P

Q

R

S